South American Mythology

LIBRARY OF THE WORLD'S MYTHS AND LEGENDS

South American Mythology

Harold Osborne

PETER BEDRICK BOOKS
NEW YORK

Half-title page. A clay figure from one of the tombs in the Cauca River valley of Colombia. The shield suggests a warrior and the slit eyes are like those of the Quimbaya gold figures; but nothing is known of the people who built the tombs, and made figures like these, about the sixth century A.D. The American Museum of Natural History, New York.

Frontispiece. The characteristic naturalism of Mochica ceramics is shown in this figure of a warrior of A.D. 1–500. Warriors appear to have enjoyed an eminent place in Mochica society.

New revised edition first published in the United States in 1986 by Peter Bedrick Books, New York.

Second impression 1988

South American Mythology first published in 1968. New revised edition published 1983 by Newnes Books, a division of The Hamlyn Publishing Group Limited. Published by agreement with The Hamlyn Publishing Group Limited.

Library of Congress Cataloging-in-Publication-Data

Osborne, Harold, 1905–
      South American Mythology.

      (Library of the world's myths and legends)
      Includes index.
      1. Indians of South America –
         Religion and mythology. I. Title.
II. Series.
F2230.1.R308   1986   299'.8   85-28567
ISBN 0-87226-043-7

Printed in Yugoslavia

Contents

Introduction

The Peoples of South America

Speculation about the origin of human beings in the Western Hemisphere has been rife ever since the discovery of America. In an age when the Old Testament was accepted as inspired history the discovery of populations in the New World raised a theological rather than a scientific problem – or at any rate a scientific problem which had to be settled within an established theological framework. The naive speculations of the early Conquistadores were inevitably committed to the traditional Biblical world-picture and had to find a place for the native peoples of America within that picture. While these wild and groping guesses are no more than a historical curiosity today, the attitude of mind which they represent is of interest to us since it was antipathetic to the serious preservation of native cosmological myths and local beliefs about origins. In so far as these were in conflict with Biblical 'truth', they were contemptuously rejected by the early chroniclers as pernicious follies and deceits of the devil. Thus a wealth of material which might have been of inestimable value to the modern student was irretrievably lost.

Only slightly later 'nativist' views were put forward which took the form of locating the Biblical Creation and the Garden of Eden in the New World. These claims have not stood up to criticism and it is now generally accepted to be pretty well beyond dispute that people first entered America by migration across the Bering Strait during the last phases of the final glacial period, probably about 20,000 B.C. At that time the ice-cap held captive vast quantities of water with the result that the sea level was three hundred feet lower than at present. Thus the present Bering Strait was a broad isthmus forming a land bridge between Asia and North America.

The native peoples of America, who were of predominantly Mongoloid stock, immigrated from the region of Siberia and slowly spread from Alaska southwards, reaching Tierra del Fuego not later than about 5,000 B.C. They brought with them the elements of a Stone Age culture, which included the use of fire, techniques of cutting and grinding bones, flint chipping, the dressing of skins and perhaps various shamanistic religious observances and rituals such as birth, puberty and death rites. It is not possible to determine over what period the waves of immigration by way of the Bering Strait continued, but we can be confident that they did not go on after the melting of the last great ice-cap. They therefore ceased before agriculture was known anywhere in the world and the hunting and food-gathering stage of development lasted in America some 10,000 to 15,000 years – or in some regions which are unsuited to agriculture virtually until the present day.

Probably between 4,000 and 3,000 B.C., at a reasonable estimate, native American plants began to be domesticated in a few areas and the three prime American food products, maize, beans and squash, spread widely over South and North America in a large number of varieties adapted to local conditions. The pastoral stage, during which the llama, alpaca and cavey or guinea-pig were domesticated for use, is thought to have been roughly contemporary. Relics of a pre-ceramic culture from about 2,500 to 1,800 B.C. have been studied chiefly in Huaca Prieta at the

mouth of the Chicama valley on the northern coast of Peru. Woven and decorated cotton textiles were found, gourds, mats and baskets of reeds and wide-meshed fish nets. Small, carved figures of equal or greater antiquity have been found farther north. From archaeological evidence a general pattern of progress in civilisation and cultural techniques has been traced for the Central Andean region from about the middle of the second millennium B.C. and extending up to the conquest of the Inca empire by the Spanish in A.D. 1532. Elsewhere in South America the patterns were widely different and less clearly marked.

There has been considerable controversy between anthropologists who believe that South American culture was in the main indigenous and others who have claimed that its basic features were derived from outside the Western Hemisphere, being carried by trans-Pacific migrations from China, Indonesia or elsewhere in the Far East. A few traditions preserved by the early Spanish chroniclers have sometimes been thought to provide evidence of such contacts. For example, Sarmiento tells a curious story

Gold pectoral from the Nariño heights of Colombia.

that in his expedition against the coast of Manta, the island of Puna and Tumbez, Topa Inca Yupanqui encountered merchants who had come over the western sea in boats and who told of two wealthy and populous islands, Ayachumbi and Ninachumbi, whence they came. After verifying their story by means of a magician, Topa Inca manned a large expedition of 20,000 men, sailed to the islands and returned with black people, much gold, a chair of brass, and the skin and jawbone of a horse. The horse's skin and jawbone were said to be still in the possession of the Inca noble who told Sarmiento the story. Such legends cannot be regarded as conclusive and together with legends of a race of white invaders and the giant invaders of Puerto Viejo might preserve memories of contacts with Northern or Central America. While today few anthropologists would deny completely the possibility of transoceanic contacts, the most authoritative opinion now is that any such cultural influences, particularly up to the Christian era, must have been at most casual and intermittent and can have exerted no important impact on the total picture of South American culture. It therefore seems most likely that the mythology of the South American peoples developed from the beliefs of the original Stone Age immigrants and was elaborated without significant influences from outside the continent up to the time of the Conquest. From the time of the Conquest there was very rapid and extensive syncretism of native mythology with Christian doctrine and to a lesser extent with European folk stories and superstitions. This fact accounts for the great importance which today is attached to the rather scanty records of native myth and legend left by the early Spanish chroniclers. Before them, in the absence of writing, nothing was recorded to indicate their religious beliefs or practices.

There have been some later studies of the mythology of particular areas or tribes. But no general study of mythology over the whole subcontinent has hitherto been attempted and even the particular and limited studies suffer from the fact that it is impossible to separate those elements which belong to the original mythological beliefs from later accretions. One may assume that the pre-Spanish mythology has survived in its most unadulterated form among the peoples who have been most isolated from European influences. For example, P. Thomas Falkner, S.J. lived among the Patagonians from 1740 to 1767 and wrote *Description of Patagonia and adjoining parts of South America* in 1774. The following remarks seem to indicate a combination of beliefs common to most of the peoples of

South America, with their emphasis on good and bad spirits, the association of spirits with particular localities and the further association with ancestors and clans. He writes: 'These Indians believe in two superior beings, one good and one bad... They imagined a multitude of these deities, one of whom presided over the destinies of each family and clan, which they thought he had created. Some call themselves the clan of the tiger, others of the lion, some the clan of the guanaco, and others the clan of the ostrich. They imagine that each one of these deities has his separate abode, in large underground caverns, beneath some lake, mountain peak, etc., and when any Indian dies his soul goes to live with the deity who presides over his family to enjoy there the felicity of a continuous and limitless inebriation... They also suppose that the stars are former Indians, that the Milky Way is the hunting ground where these Indians chase ostriches, that the two southern clouds are the feathers of these ostriches whirling around... They recognise the existence of an infinite number of these demons in the world and to these they attribute every evil which occurs in the world to man or to beasts...'

Interesting for the same reason is the account of the Tupari, a tribe of Indians who until 1948 had continued virtually free from contacts with outside civilisations. (See pp. 118–24.) Among modern ethnologists who have studied the mythology of particular areas are: Rigoberto Paredes: *Mitos y Supervivencias Populares de Bolivia* (1963); Julio Vicuña Cifuentes. *Mitos y Supersticiones* (1947); Oscar Alborto Velasco: *En la Ruta de Ñuflo de Chaves* (1953); Enrique Oblitas Poblete: *Cultura Callawaya* (1978); Luiz da Carnara Cascudo (Ed.): *Mitos Brazileiros*.

It is the object of this book to present a sample of what is known about the mythological beliefs of the aboriginal peoples throughout South America. While certain striking parallels and similarities among the mythologies of distant and culturally diverse peoples will leap to the eye,

wide generalisations must at this stage of our knowledge be avoided.

Nevertheless in order to bring some order into what might otherwise appear a chaotic hotch-potch of haphazard and random variations it will be convenient to suggest some general cultural classification as a background to structures of mythological belief. For this purpose we will adapt the classification proposed by Julian H. Steward, editor of the Smithsonian *Handbook of South American Indians*. We shall omit the Circum-Caribbean peoples, who for our purposes are classed with the Central American areas, and we shall place the Southern Andean tribes in a separate category. This gives a fourfold classification into Marginal and Semi-Marginal tribes; Tropical Forest peoples; Southern Andean tribes; and Central Andean civilisations.

Marginal Tribes

These occupied comparatively unproductive regions, which they exploited by simple technologies. Hunters and food-gatherers without developed agriculture, they were frequently

Opposite left. Pottery figure of a man carrying a foal. It is probably a llama, one of the few animals of the South American continent suitable for domestication. It originated in the Altiplano but its cultivation spread rapidly when its value as a draught animal was realised. The skin was only used after the creature died and its working life was rarely more than ten years duration. Chimu culture.

Opposite right. One of the large flat unshaped stone slabs carved with large human figures and heads in outline relief engraving, found at the Cerro Séchin, in the valley of the Casma. Although apparently contemporary with the Chavín culture, they follow a different tradition of stylisation. The figure in this representation holds before him a staff of office or a ceremonial axe and has certain affinities with the running figures in the frieze of the Gate of the Sun at Tiahuanaco.

Right. The art of the Mochica potters found inspiration in every walk of life. This stirrup vessel, showing a twisted, scarred face is believed to represent a beggar.

Above. Double-spouted ceramic vessel painted with a jaguar figure combining human with feline features. This may indicate a cult figure. Nazca period. Museum Rietberg, Zurich.

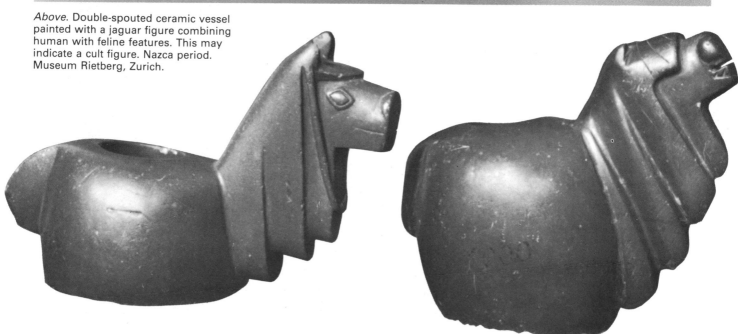

Above. Camayura Indians of the Xingú River of Brazil. The tribes of the Amazon basin were well used to river travel and it is likely that there was some trading contact between them and the Andean civilisations. But the way of life of the river people would seem to have changed little over the centuries. The Camayura are a healthy and vigorous tribe of hunters, and are seen here preparing for a wrestling game which is their favourite sport.

Below. Three stone vessels in the form of alpacas. Like the llama this animal originated in the Altiplano, and was prized for the long abundant wool. Shearing took place two or three times a year. Inca period.

nomadic or semi-nomadic and their social units were generally small and unstable, varying in size and permanency according to subsistence conditions but without uniform pattern. Their material culture remained rudimentary and they lacked the more advanced manufacturing processes found elsewhere in South America such as weaving, building and ceramic techniques, and the domestication of animals, except where – as in parts of the Chaco – these were borrowed from more advanced peoples.

Their religious outlook had a broadly similar structure based on shamanism, though with innumerable local variations of particular features. Specific magical practices, witchcraft procedures, devices for controlling the spirit world and concepts of the supernatural varied from tribe to tribe. Crisis rites and magical practices played an important role but there was no organised priesthood or social cult. Although magico-religious rites were used in some areas to control sickness or the weather, in general these peoples were without group ceremonies and rituals. Among the Archipelagic tribes of the extreme south and those of Patagonia and the Pampas there is now believed to be clear evidence of an aboriginal belief in a Supreme God, although lesser spirits – particularly spirits of evil – played a more prominent role in practical everyday life and the Supreme Deity was not the object of an organised cult. Among the tribes of the upper Xingú, the Nambicuara of western Brazil bordering the Guaporé river and the northern Ge groups there was a belief in a creator-god, sometimes identified with the sun or moon, but whether this belief was aboriginal or derivative cannot be determined. The Bororo and certain tribes of eastern Bolivia attached great importance to the spirits of the dead, who were supposed to be invisibly present at mortuary ceremonies, and some believed that the spirit-helper of the shaman was the soul of a dead shaman.

We believe it to be probable, though it is certainly not provable, that the attitudes of belief towards the supernatural which prevailed among the Marginal peoples, and the rather elementary and unembroidered mythological structure which was generally associated with it, may have remained closest to that of the Stone Age immigrants who first populated the Americas and may have undergone least differentiation from the aboriginal structure of belief. If this is so, the pattern of myth and supernatural lore found among the Marginal tribes may be regarded as a primitive foundation upon which the more complicated mythological systems of other peoples were elaborated. Any such theory must be

treated with the utmost caution since the basis of cultural classification is at best highly arbitrary, representing a compromise between socio-political features, levels of material culture and magico-religious elements, and also because the nature and extent of influences from one area to another in the matter of mythology and belief can only be conjectured.

Above. A grave discovered in the sand near the mouth of the River Loa in northern Chile. The practice of interment in deep sandy graves was common to all the peoples of the coast, among the unknown race represented here no less than the sophisticated cultures to the north. The body was put into a coarse cloth with simple belongings, the whole being wrapped before burial in the skin of a sea-lion.

Left. A man of the Suyá tribe from the Xingú river. He wears a large lip disk as well as the ubiquitous ear-plugs.

Opposite. A party of Indians on a fishing trip in the small canoes used for local travel. The great rivers served the Indians of the tropical rain-forest and the Amazon basin as highways; travel by canoe was highly developed.

Tropical Forest Peoples

These comprise in the main the tribes who inhabited the tropical rain-forests of Guiana, the Amazon basin, the Paraná delta and the area watered by the Paraguay. They developed advanced techniques of agriculture by the slash-and-burn method, which necessitated periodical movement within an area. They had more advanced exploitation devices than the Marginal tribes and utilised the rivers for transport in dug-out canoes. They cultivated tropical root crops and built frame houses with thatch. Though they lacked wool, metal and stone and were without domesticated animals, they had developed techniques of loom weaving, basketry, bark cloth and ceramics. Their social units were larger and more stable, often including large and semi-permanent villages, but they lacked political federations and empires.

The structure of religious belief remained in general similar to that of the Marginal peoples, being centred on the shaman who, with an invisible supernatural helper, controlled magical practices, cured the sick, performed functions of prognostication and divination and in general safeguarded tribal tradition, particularly in regard to the relations of the living with the world of the supernatural. Crisis rituals were important for defining social status, differentiating the functions of the sexes, and so on. There were no temples or idols and few of the Tropical Forest tribes had tribal gods or public religious ceremonies. The principle deities and celestial beings were mythological personages rather than objects of cult. The main mythological beings were personifications of the sun, the moon, the stars, thunder or rain, and some anthropologists believe these to have been the prototypes of the tribal deities of the Andean peoples. Belief in a multitude of nature spirits was general, though spirits of mountains, streams, rocks, springs and place spirits in general seem to have been less important than they were among the more settled peoples of the Andes. Belief in a supernatural jaguar spirit or were-jaguar was widespread in some areas, surviving until very recent times in parts of eastern Bolivia, and may have been the source of a jaguar cult in the Central Andes.

Southern Andean Tribes

These comprise chiefly the peoples of the Atacama desert, the Diaguita of northern Argentina and of the states of Atacama and Coquimbo in Chile, and the Araucanians of central Chile. In socio-political structure and perhaps in popular religious belief their culture had affinities with the peoples of the Tropical Forest. But in material aspects it was closer to that of the Central Andes. They shared with the Central Andes techniques of metallurgy, building in stone, breeding of llamas, and wore Andean types of clothing. Their agricultural techniques were also Andean, based on the cultivation of the potato and of cereals such as maize and quinoa.

During the expansion of the Inca empire, and perhaps even before, strong cultural influences spread directly from the Central Andes to northern Argentina and Chile. Over large parts of the Chaco direct influences from the Central Andes overlapped with those from the Tropical Forest peoples of Brazil.

There is little evidence of organised priesthood or temple religion among the Southern Andean peoples apart from agricultural ceremonies. The Diaguita conducted agricultural ceremonies and the Atacameño had fertility rites for their fields. The Araucanians had a public ceremony conducted by priests who said prayers and offered animal sacrifices to a Supreme Being and creator-god for good crops and the health of the people. These public ceremonials may well have grown up under influences from the Central Andes and we know little in detail about them. The religion of the Araucanians in particular seems to have been dominated by belief in witchcraft, magic and by the propitiation of ill-disposed supernatural beings. Shamans were important and the Araucanian shaman was a transvestite. Shamans used divination, cured disease and brought rain. Diseases were thought to be caused by the intrusion of some foreign object, possession by an evil spirit, by magic or ill-wishing, or by the loss of a man's soul. The shaman obtained his powers in the supernatural realm, among them magical and curative powers, from association with a dead shamanistic helper

and also from the Supreme Being, to whom he offered prayers.

Central Andean Civilisations

The most advanced civilisation of the subcontinent of South America was developed in the Central Andean region, roughly coextensive with the territories of the modern Bolivia and Peru. It was centred in the coastal valleys of Peru, the high valleys which seam the western slopes of the Cordillera and the rather bleak and arid plateau which is now known as the Altiplano. It was a civilisation based on agriculture: semi-tropical fruits and root crops in the hot coastal valleys, maize and other cereals in the highland valleys, and potatoes and quinoa on the high plateau. The llama, the alpaca, the guinea-pig and the duck were domesticated; other animals were preserved and hunted. Specialised agricultural techniques were developed, including large-scale irrigation systems and terracing, and agricultural surpluses were produced which supported the densest aggregations of population found anywhere in the Americas and allowed for large non-productive classes of nobility, priesthood and warriors. Mechanical processes of production in the crafts were brought to a level which has been surpassed nowhere in the world before the age of machine manufacture and the aesthetic quality of the work was such that surviving examples have a place of honour in museums and collections throughout the world today. Agricultural and manufacturing processes developed in the Central Andes spread southwards into northern Argentina, the fringe of the Chaco and northern Chile; to the north they permeated into Central America and Mexico; and from the Caribbean they were carried down the Atlantic coast and up the great rivers to leave their mark here and there among the tribes of the Tropical Forest area. It is not unreasonable to suppose that elements of myth and legend were disseminated along with the spread of trade and manufacturing processes.

Although the mountainous nature of the terrain made for scattered population centres, this was the only part of South America which developed a civilisation on a genuinely urban pattern. Society was organised on a stratified basis with kings, nobility, priesthood and classes based on occupation. Unlike the rest of South America, unification over large areas was effected by military conquest resulting in permanent domination and empire. The basis of social organisation was the land-owning village community, the *ayllu*, a settlement cemented on grounds of kinship. In the earlier stages of development there were important centres of religious pilgrimage and cultural dissemination at Chavín de Huantar in northern Peru, at Tiahuanaco on the borders of Lake Titicaca in northern Bolivia and at Pachacamac near Lima. During the so-called 'Urbanist' period, from about A.D. 1000, important urban centres were built. The powerful coastal kingdom of Chimu had its capital at Chanchan, near the present city of Trujillo, and the still impressive ruins cover an area of eight square miles. Cuzco, the highland capital of the Inca empire, based on military conquest, extended a unitary social organisation and administration from northern Ecuador to the river Maule in Chile.

There are several good and easily accessible accounts of the Central Andean civilisations of South America. We shall restrict ourselves here to giving some details of the structure of religious belief and ceremonial which have most relevance to mythology. But readers of popular and unscientific literature about pre-columbian South America should exercise the utmost caution in view of the extreme hazards which beset historical reconstructions based on archaeological material alone without written records – and the art of writing was nowhere practised in South America. How closely population movements or social developments can be correlated with changes in artistic styles or manipulative techniques is a matter of speculation where exact verification is virtually impossible.

In the field of mythology and religious belief the difficulties are still more serious. Without outside clues in the form of written records or comparisons with closely related cultures where the significance is known, it is not possible to determine the nature of religious belief from surviving cult

---

Opposite. The Altiplano, with its forsaken aspect of a landscape on some vaster and more ancient planet where life has long been obsolete. It is a harsh, inhuman land, inhabited now by a dour, unsmiling, toiling race; a high, bleak, barren, windswept tundra with the paradox of a tropical sun blazing through the frigid air. Yet the Altiplano was the home of the greatest civilisations and cultures which South America has known: the Tiahuanaco culture and later the Inca. It was the Collasuyu of the ancient Inca empire and the Collao of the Spaniards. It runs roughly north to south at an elevation of 12,000 to 13,000 feet above sea level from northern Peru to the southern tip of Bolivia, a distance of 520 miles, and averages eighty to a hundred miles across. There are no trees and except during the brief season of the rains there is no green.

Below. Chimu gold figurine wearing fan-type headdress.

15

Left. Detail of the central wall decoration from one of the two Chanchan palaces, showing a stylised bird pattern. According to Hermann Leicht, the historian of the Chimu civilisation, the walls of the palace courtyards 'were covered with fine white plaster painted with vivid scenes such as one can still admire today on much of the pottery. Other walls were covered with geometrical arabesques, chequered and rhomboid patterns as well as complicated patterns in severely hieratic style, reminiscent not only of Tiahunaco but . . . of the burial city of the Zapotec kings'.

Below. Relief from the Chanchan ruins, perhaps depicting a man performing a ritual ceremony. In the absence of contemporary records it has proved impossible to derive from these reliefs any specific facts of mythological or religious beliefs among the Chimu.

Bottom. Relief from Chanchan; an example of the patterns which approach the complicated symbolism which, from the Chavín times to the Nazca, features in the design of sculptured figures and of painted pottery.

17

Gold was a favourite medium for decorative and ritual objects throughout the civilisation of Peru, and further north. A considerable amount has survived the devastations of the Conquistadores and subsequent looters. *Above*. Gold mask from Iquitos, perhaps intended as a Sun figure with rays terminating in snake heads. Nazca period. Señor Mujico Gallo, Lima. *Right* Gold dish worked in repoussé, depicting the Earth Goddess together with maize, juccaa, sweet potatoes, etc. in sections representing the seasons of sowing. Chimu period. Señor Mujico Gallo, Lima. *Opposite*. Gold plaque in the form of a puma with a human face depicted on the tongue and pendants in the shape of ceremonial kines hanging from the ears. Mochica period. Señor Mujico Gallo, Lima.

On page 16. Tambo Colorado, on the desert plain of Peru. The building here was accomplished without the stone so readily available in the highlands but equal skill was shown in the use of adobe bricks. In the desert air the colours have lasted and much of the decoration can be seen in its original state. Inca culture.

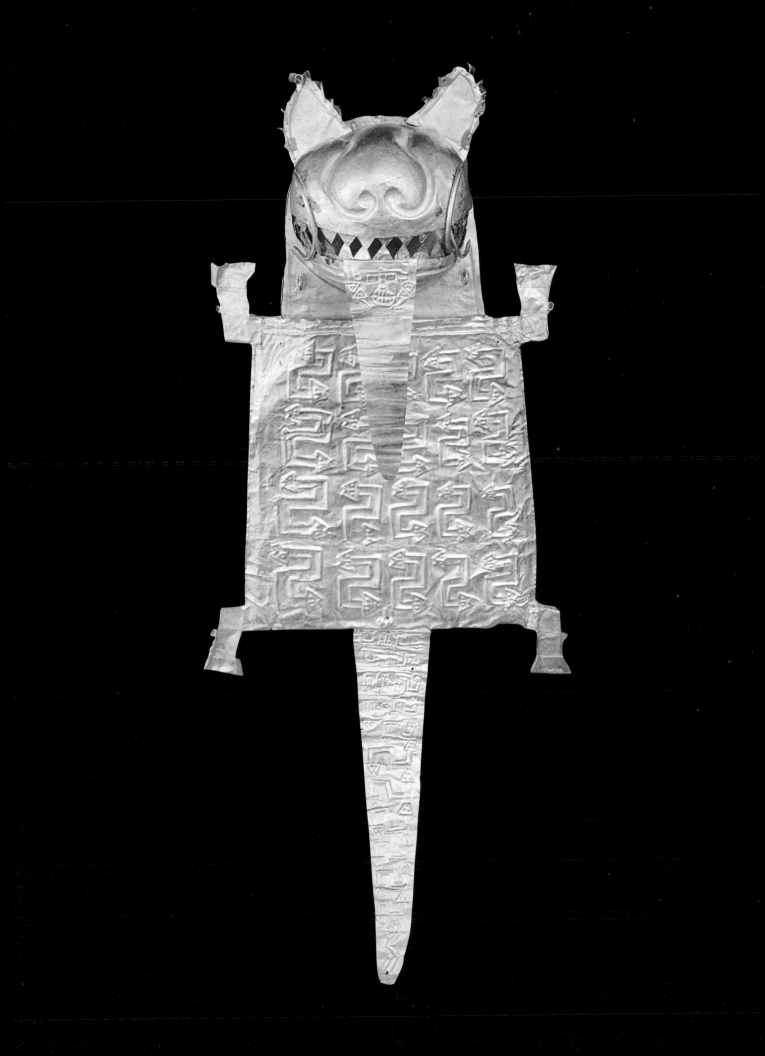

Above. Chanchan, capital of the Chimu kingdom, the ruins of which lie to the north of the Moche river, not far from the modern town of Trujillo. The name Chimu is given to the most splendid of the coastal kingdoms of Peru preceding the rise to power of the highland Inca. At the time of its greatest expansion, from about A.D. 100 to 1400, Chimu was the dominant power over a strip of land stretching 600 miles along the coast, from the river Chicama to the Patavilca valley and reaching inland 30 to 100 miles, to include, among others, the highland valleys of Recuay and Huaras. The kernel of the Chimu kingdom was the extensive and fertile valley of the Chicama. The imposing ruins of the walled capital, Chanchan, cover an area of some eight square miles. There are relics of innumerable canals and aqueducts leading to city squares in which once were large gardens and green parks, as well as extensive harbour installations, now well above the tide mark.

Top left. Relief from Chanchan: one of many giving evidence of an intense and alert preoccupation with the limited fauna – feline, snake, fox, falcon, condor, guinea-pig, badger and marine animals. The method of stylisation and the expressive impact made by the conventionalised patterns seem to indicate a religious as well as an aesthetic interest.

Top right. Stone lintel found at Chavín de Huántar carved with a crude and semi-naturalistic representation of a feline figure – the puma, jaguar or mountain cat which is the most frequent motif in Chavín art and which archaeologists regard as evidence of a feline cult, though snakes, condors and other animals are also used in designs. The feline's broad flat nose, staring eyes, claw feet and square mouth of grinning teeth with overlapping fangs are all typical of what was later stylised into a convention which was taken up by the Paracas and Nazca and perpetuated into and through Inca times.

objects or to derive the content of myths from pictorial representations. All attempts to do so must remain purely subjective and unverifiable. Indeed it is never possible in these circumstances to be certain that an artistic representation or motif has in fact a religious significance, or to be certain that the subject of a pictorial scene has any relation whatever to myth or legend.

The dangers of basing mythological reconstructions on archaeological evidence may be illustrated by the following difficulties. They are illustrations only of a very general problem. Students of archaeology tend to take it as more or less certain that the Chavín culture was predominantly religious in character and that the cult of a feline deity, perhaps also a condor-deity and a snake-deity, spread widely over the coastal area of Peru. Yet the surviving records from the early years of the Conquest, sparse as they are, afford little or no support for such cults. The records do suggest the worship of a supreme creator-deity who may have been named Con or Viracocha, but the archaeological material provides no evidence which could with reasonable probability be ascribed to this cult. The very elaborate burial customs – almost all our archaeological material has been recovered from burials – might well lead one to suppose that there must have been a fairly well developed mythology of the after-life. Yet the records which survive are extremely meagre on this matter. The sculptures at Tiahuanaco and the highly formalised relief carvings and artistic motifs have led archaeologists to suppose a well-organised religious control for this culture, which spread – perhaps by conquest – to the coastal areas of Peru from the Bolivian highlands.

However, though the Spanish chroniclers who visited the area in the early years after the Conquest gathered some elements of indigenous Aymará mythology from the local inhabitants, they gleaned nothing which could throw light on the religious or mythological significance of Tiahuanaco. It is not until Inca times

that we can get a more detailed picture based on surviving memories of cult and myths. It is for this reason that the study of South American mythology, if it aspires to be more than a subjective fancy picture, must depend almost entirely on written records (or on the field researches of ethnologists in more modern times), even though these are very scanty, for some of the most interesting areas and times.

In the religion of the highland farmers, the village communities or *ayllus*, animistic beliefs, sorcerers and medicine-men were most prominent. Crisis events in the life of the individual were treated as family affairs rather than as matters of public ritual. The major communal religious ceremonies and rituals were connected with the agricultural cycle and many of these have persisted in a reduced form until the present. They were systematised and elaborated by the Inca and we have fairly detailed accounts by Cristóbal de Molina, Felipe Guamán Poma de Ayala and others of the early chroniclers. Popular religion was dominated by the conception of the *huaca*, which meant basically anything at all which was supposed to be holy or fraught with spiritual force, or the dwelling place of a spirit. *Huacas* varied enormously from household fetishes, charms, any strange or unusual objects, to temples and symbols of the gods, things to do with the cult of the dead, and objects important in tribal tradition such as the shrine of Ayar Ucho at Huanacauri and the stone relic of Ayar Auca which became the field-guardian of Cuzco and the stones from the battle-field where the Inca defeated the Chanca, which in Inca legend were supposed to have been turned into men to aid the forces of Cusi Inca Yupanqui.

Huacas of locality were particularly important in the highland religion. They might be mountains, springs, trees, caves or any other natural feature. A particular class were the cairns of stones, called *apachitas*, which even today are built up by travellers at dangerous spots or at the highest point of a road. The

preservation of the bodies of ancestors or founders of the clan, dried and half-mummified by the cold air of the highland plateau, was a general feature. In the four years from 1615 to 1619, according to a letter from Francisco de Borja to the King of Spain, the Spaniards took from the Indians of Peru 1,365 such 'mummies of ancestors'. The bodies of the dead Inca were preserved and became the objects of a cult. Even today the word *huaca* is in general popular use for anything connected with an ancient burial, as for example the textiles and ceramics which find their way into museums and private collections.

During a period lasting roughly from 850 to 400 B.C. the art products of the coastal and highland valleys of Peru were dominated by a style and motifs which spread from the temple site of Chavín de Huantar in northern Peru and this has led to the supposition that the cultural advances which took place in these centuries were associated with a religious movement superimposed on the amorphous local cults. It is thought that Chavín was a centre of pilgrimage and that associated with it was the worship of tribal deities, with some form of organised priesthood and temple cult, in the shape of a feline (jaguar) deity, a condor, a snake and possibly certain fish deities. The evidence is entirely archaeological and nothing in detail is known about the nature of the beliefs associated with the cult or the mythological background.

Our ignorance of the nature of the highland religion which centred on Tiahuanaco is almost as great. Even the dates are uncertain. Some authorities place the Tiahuanaco period from about 300 B.C. to about A.D. 500, others from about A.D. 400 to about A.D. 1000. The little we know about the highland Aymará mythology does not bear an obvious or close relation to the Tiahuanaco religion as manifested in archaeological remains.

We know more about the Inca religion. It was a hierarchical theocratic state religion based on the principle of divine kingship. The Sun was the tribal god of the Inca aristocracy and the Inca monarchs were personifications, representatives, or 'sons' of the sun-god. The religion also recognised a creator-god Viracocha, a moon-god, gods of stars and weather – in particular the god of thunder – and a host of minor gods and spirits. In relation to conquered peoples the Inca adopted the system of syncretism and absorption, bringing their local deities and cults within the organised state religion, so that it becomes almost impossible to disentangle genuine Inca features from syncretistic elements. Even the basic Inca mythology and cult seem to have been largely borrowed or linked with the highland sun-worship (possibly part of the Tiahuanaco religion) which centred upon Lake Titicaca. The Inca state religion was highly organised, with temple worship, a priestly class, elaborate rituals to cover almost every aspect of life, a class of Sacred Virgins of the Sun, rites of confession, penitence, excommunication, and so on. It did not suppress the more primitive *huaca* religion, and did not make much inroad on the widely spread beliefs in sorcery and magic, but was a superimposed national cult and ritual fostering the divine majesty of the Inca monarchs and their empire.

Opposite. Polychrome pottery jar from Pachacamac, showing Tiahuanaco influence. The neck is in the form of a stylised human head with headdress and the body is decorated with conventionalised symbols of animal forms. Pachacamac, on a hill near present-day Lima, was the site of a famous temple and cult centre of the god Viracocha. The enormous value of the offerings deposited there by worshippers in pre-Inca and Inca times excited the greed of the Spanish invaders.

Below. A mask of beaten gold from one of the Nazca graves. The shape of this funerary offering suggests devotion to the cult of the sun, but neither the remarkably beautiful Nazca ceramics nor the accomplished use of weaving techniques offers a positive answer. Knowledge of this culture only dates from 1901, when it was discovered by Max Uhle.

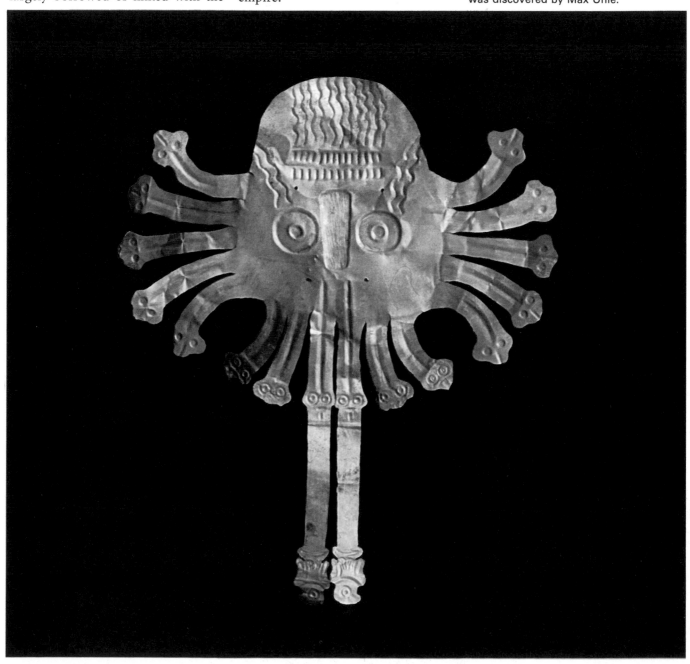

Sources for Mythology

Tribal history, legend and the background of mythology were preserved by word of mouth, and among the more organised peoples special classes of professional historians and reciters were fostered. As the Inca extended their conquests their ubiquitous passion for organisation did not

---

Right. Common to all the great pre-columbian cultures was a genius for construction. This detail from the ruins of Machu Picchu shows the extraordinarily fine stonework found in the great Inca sites, where huge blocks were held together by the precision in fitting – no mortar was used.

Below. An Inca record-keeper using his *quipu*, a string from which hung down variously coloured cords. By means of knots tied at different intervals in the various cords and by different methods of twisting and differences in the size and kind of knot, the Inca and other South American peoples used the *quipu* as a mnemonic device. It could be used not only for statistical, calendrical and other records, but also as a reminder of verses memorised to perpetuate the record of history and events. Thus, though writing was unknown to the peoples of South America before the conquest, among the more stable cultures of the Central Andes legends, traditions and mythology were preserved over many generations.
Drawing by Guamán Poma de Ayala.

neglect the structuring of history and legend. In some cases they combined and syncretised, adopting myth and legend of subject peoples as their own; in other cases they suppressed. They exercised a deliberate and systematic policy of distorting recorded history by obliterating the achievements of their predecessors in the advancement of civilisation, truncating the remembered traditions and representing themselves – or their legendary tribal ancestors – as the original bearers and inventors of culture to peoples living at a pre-agricultural stage of hunting and food-gathering, without manufacturing crafts or social organisation. From the official Inca corpus of legend the contributions of the coastal peoples – the Chavín culture and the great

coastal kingdoms which followed it – and of the southern highland peoples, the megalithic builders of Tiahuanaco, have disappeared.

We depend for our knowledge of myth and legend, even in this systematically distorted form, entirely on the records of the chroniclers who wrote during the early decades after the Conquest. In general they lacked the objective and scientific interest which we have today, and even the sort of impartial curiosity which is nowadays taken for granted was rare among them. Some were genuinely eager to find out what the Indians themselves believed about their origins and took the trouble to question Indian authorities and record what they said. In some cases their motive was to justify the destructive Spanish occupa-

tion by showing that the Inca themselves had held their domination by conquest and not by right. Others had a less partial interest. But all were hampered by a rigid belief in the literal truth of Biblical records and a horror of anything which conflicted with Christian dogma. As we have said, owing to this reason a great deal of mythological and legendary material which we should have valued today was contemptuously passed by in silence as trivial or immoral. Again and again our sources stop short just at the point where we should have found the continuation of most interest.

The few Indian or half-Indian chroniclers wrote under a strong impulse to assert their Christian orthodoxy and were inclined to emphasise aspects of native mythology which seemed to parallel Christian doctrine. With the exception of the mestizo Garcilaso Inca de la Vega, who wrote many years later in Spain, these native chroniclers were not men of high education, and were poorly versed in the language. Moreover, as is usual wherever tradition depends on oral memory and is not yet fixed by written records, the mythopoeic faculty was still active and there is no doubt that from the very early years of the Conquest the local mythology and legends were conflated with and coloured by the Christian teachings of the missionaries. This is particularly noticeable with the Thunupa legends which were gathered somewhat later by Spanish missionaries who had settled on the Altiplano.

Outside the Central Andean region our early knowledge depends in the main on the records made by the Jesuits who extended their missions over the tribes of the upper Amazon, eastern Bolivia, the province of Chiquitos, the Chaco, Paraguay and the Pampas, and who were particularly successful with the Guarani Indians of the middle and upper Paraguay and Uruguay rivers. Their descriptions of the cultures of the Indians whom they converted are invaluable and are often scientific and objective in character. Some useful information about mythological beliefs is embedded in these descriptions, but here too it is often difficult to determine the extent to which the original material has been conflated with the new Christian teaching. The desire of the Indian to please causes him to adapt his account to his hearer.

Myth, Legend and Folklore

The anthropologist Bronislaw Malinowski once said: 'Myth is the constant by-product of a living faith in need of miracles, of sociological status which demands precedent, of moral rule which demands sanction.' Myths are often more or less closely linked with religious beliefs and cults, social customs including crisis and other rites, and magical and medicinal lore. In addition to genuine myth South American cultures contained a great wealth of folk story,

including animal stories of all kinds, and an abundance of legendary material, much of which embodies confused traditions of tribal movements or the emergence and decline of cultures and technologies. It is not possible to make any precise line of demarcation between folk story, legend and myth, and indeed a great deal of the material which has survived combines features of each. In the following survey no attempt has been made to cover South American folk story, legend or religious belief as such; but myth elements have not been excluded simply in the interests of academic preciseness because they incorporate features which belong more properly to legend or story. For example, the myths of Inca origins, which rank among the most interesting of the Central Andean material, have the appearance of incorporating a considerable body of legend artificially conflated with earlier legendary and genuine mythological cycles.

Nowhere in South American cultures do we find an elaborate polytheistic mythology associated with a divine pantheon such as the Olympic deities of the Greeks and the animal-shaped gods of Egypt. The innumerable ghostly and supernatural powers by which men's lives were swayed belonged in the realm of popular or organised occultism and were not so highly personalised as to attract genuine mythological cycles. On the other hand cultural and causal myth was more fully developed, and cycles on the borderland between myth and legend were cherished and preserved through the generations. Mythological pictures about the after-life are not well developed among the advanced civilisations and among the more primitive cultures are little elaborated beyond the bounds of folk story. Perhaps the most ubiquitous features in South American myth are the stories of a deluge and variant accounts of the origins of advanced agricultural and social cultures with or without a divine culture hero. It is, however, difficult to determine how far such generalisations belong to the original character of the mythological material and how far they are

accounted for by the conditions of preservation.

For the sake of convenience South American myth may be classified into the following categories.

The origin of the world. Myths of the origins of the universe are not well developed. Apart from infrequent stories of fabulous mythological animals, the origin of the sun and constellations is usually attributed to a creator-god and often connected with a deluge.

The deluge. Myths of a deluge are very widespread among both the highland peoples and the tribes of the tropical lowlands. The deluge is commonly connected with the creation and with an epiphany of the creator-god. It is often associated with the creation of the human race or of the present tribes. It is sometimes regarded as a divine punishment wiping out existing humankind in preparation for the emergence of a new race.

The creation of the human race. The origin of human beings as they are now is commonly attributed to the act of a creator-god and often connected with the deluge. Some mythological cycles feature a primitive age of darkness before the existence of the sun, when human beings lived in a state of anarchy without the techniques of civilised life. Sometimes myths in this category appear to embody a confused racial memory of a hunting and food-gathering stage. It is not uncommon for them to be associated with a tradition of the destruction of the primitive food-gathering race by a creator-god and the creation of new races, usually following a deluge. In the mythology both of the highland peoples and of the tropical forest tribes the creation of the present human race is very frequently connected with natural features, such as mountains, rivers and caverns or even trees and rocks, in a way which appears to indicate a close relation with the animistic religion of *huacas*, or the worship of natural features, which preceded the more organised cults of national divinities but persisted alongside them.

The culture hero. Myths of a culture hero who brought the arts of

civilisation to the present races of mankind are often connected, as in the official Inca myth, with the legendary ancestor of a tribe. Sometimes the culture hero is identified with the creator-god. The creator was also called Pachayachachic, meaning Teacher of the World, in Peru. More often he is represented as the semi-divine son of the creator or as a human being with miraculous powers. His appearance generally follows the deluge and the creation of the races.

Aetiological myths. Myths purporting to explain the origin of tribes, dynasties, religious or magical rituals, animals, unusual natural features, social institutions and the like are to be found throughout the continent. Indeed all myths of the foregoing categories tend to take on an aetiological character.

In addition there is a great wealth of folklore, including stories which conform to the world-wide type of animal story illustrating the typical characteristics of various species of animal life, and there is an abundance of legendary material, much of which incorporates confused traditions of the movements of tribes or the emergence and decline of cultures. It is not possible to make any precise line of division between folk story, legend and myth. As will be apparent, the myths themselves do not fall clearly into one or the other of the above categories but almost always combine features from several. In quoting the myths, therefore, as reported by the ancient chroniclers or the ethnologists it is not possible to arrange them in the categories as defined. The great majority of reports will be seen to bring together elements from several categories and this is undoubtedly the way in which the mythology has survived in native tradition.

Opposite. A highland Indian depicted on a glazed vase of the Mochica culture which flourished on the north coast of Peru, A.D. 400 – 1000. The Quechua Indian of today (*below*), here seen playing a *quena* flute, is distinctly of the same race. The Quechuas are the same people who, under the lead of the Incas, achieved greatness with the empire which the Conquistadores plundered in the sixteenth century.

The Divine Origin of the Inca

We begin with the myths of Inca origins both because these have been recorded most frequently and in some cases most carefully by the early chroniclers, and also because when mythological material of greater antiquity survives it has often come down to us conflated with Inca legend. Indeed the official Inca accounts of their legendary origins may fairly be surmised to have taken their shape largely by the appropriation of folk stories which long antedated the rise of their dynasty.

There are three main legends of Inca origins. They all contain a large admixture of mythical elements and all establish a claim for a special relationship of the Inca nobility to the sun-deity. The Inca monarchs expanded and stabilised their empire with an organising genius and technological brilliance not inferior to that of the Romans. The social system which they imposed was based on the hierarchical principle of divine kingship, and the prestige of their authority went hand in hand with the cult of the Sun which they propagated. At the pinnacle of the hierarchy were the Inca rulers, who were themselves worshipped as children of the Sun. The mythical origins of the dynasty confirmed and supported this cult. It will be seen that many of the details of the stories incidentally provided a rationale for Inca institutions and rituals, e.g. the marriage of the reigning monarch to a sister, the cult of Huanacauri.

The first version tells of a cliff with three small cave mouths, or a building with three exits, about twenty miles from the present city of Cuzco. It was called Paccari-tambo (Inn of Origin) or Tambotocco (Place of the Hole). In prehistoric times four brothers and four sisters, who were to be the founders of the Inca dynasty, emerged from the middle orifice. Their names and numbers are differently given – according to some versions the ancestors of other, non-royal Inca clans emerged from the other two orifices. These brothers and sisters differed in costume and appearance from the local population and were able to gain a moral ascendancy over them. They proceeded slowly in the general direction of Cuzco, looking for good land on which to settle. One of the brothers, Ayar Cachi, incurred the resentment of the others by his feats of strength and his boastfulness. In particular he climbed to the top of a mountain, Huanacauri, and hurling stones from his sling at the neighbouring hills, he opened up ravines where none had been before. The brothers therefore induced him to return to the cave to fetch objects which they had left behind and walled him up inside it. The other brothers went on and made a temporary settlement at Tambu Quiru. Here they were visited miraculously by the spirit of Ayar Cachi, who after exhorting them to proceed with the foundation of Cuzco turned himself to stone on the hill Huanacauri and became the object of a later Inca cult. According to another version it was the brother Ayar Ucho who, after instructing Manco Capac in the maturity ritual for Inca youths, turned to stone on Huanacauri. Manco Capac (or Ayar Manco) went on with the sisters until they eventually reached the site of Cuzco. Here they found the terrain suitable to their needs and, after driving off the Indian

Opposite. Stirrup jar with the modelled head of a fox wearing a cap and ear plugs. North coast *c.* A.D. 1–750.

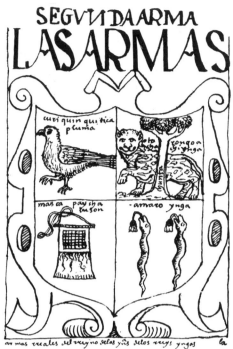

tribe which was settled there, they founded their city. Manco Capac with his wife and sister Mama Ocllo were the first rulers.

The idea of human ancestors emerging from rocks and caves is common among the peoples of South America. The story of brothers – often involved in fratricidal strife – as cultural heroes or founders of the tribe is also very widely disseminated and is met far beyond the Central Andean area. The Inca may have taken over and adapted the story from local folklore or they may have furbished up a legend which had been perpetuated from more ancient times in their tribe.

In a second version the sun-god, seeing men living in a state of primitive barbarity, felt pity for them and sent to earth on an island in Lake Titicaca his two children Manco Capac and Mama Ocllo, brother and sister, to instruct them in the arts of civilised life. These two journeyed northwards over the Altiplano carrying with them a long golden rod, and were to settle when they came to a place where the rod could be buried entirely in the soil. (In a region where for the most part the earth is thin, stony and unprolific the test for deep and penetrable soil makes sense.) When they reached the valley of

Cuzco (a highland valley some 11,000 ft above sea level) they first stopped at Huanacauri. Proceeding further, they came to the site of Cuzco, where the rod sank into the ground. Here they founded the city as the seat of their empire, won over the native peoples by teaching them the arts of civilisation, and instituted the religion of the sun.

This version of Inca origins bears a close affinity with a common form of creation myth. Creation – or at any rate the origin of civilisation – seems to have been linked with the story of a flood (see p. 30). Before the flood people lived in a state of primitive barbarity. After the world had been destroyed by the flood the creator brought into being a new race and sent down to earth a culture hero to teach them the arts of civilisation. In the Inca version the sun-god takes the place of (or is closely linked with) the creator, and the founders of the Inca race are depicted as culture heroes, assuming the characteristics of divine agents who elsewhere bear other names such as Viracocha or Thunupa or Pachacamac. The Inca myth is obviously conflated most nearly with the creation story in the southern Altiplano and ties up the origin of the Inca with the sacred Lake Titicaca in whose basin stood Tiahuanaco,

which was the capital of an earlier religious culture.

One effect of this version was to suppress the memory of the important pre-Inca culture and to represent the Inca as universal benefactors who brought civilisation and culture to the whole of the human race. Among modern Indian peoples of the highlands the Inca themselves have become a subject of myth and legend.

According to a third version, Inca divine kingship originated in an astute deception practised by an early Inca king, who dressed himself in a shining cloak of gold or beads and, parading before his ignorant subjects, so impressed them with his majesty in the glittering rays of the sun that they were prepared to worship him as the offspring and representative of the sun-god. Some chroniclers, for example Ramos Gavilan in his *Historia del célebre Santuario de Nuestra Señora de Copacabana*, published in Lima in 1621, and Martín de Morúa in this century, tell this story of the first Inca king, Manco Capac. Others

Left. A drawing by Guamán Poma de Ayala which shows the Inca and his queen ceremoniously acknowledging the origins of their race and of the royal house at Paccari-Tambo (Inn of Origin) or Tambotocco (Place of the Hole) as it was variously called.

Opposite left and centre. The Inca royal arms, according to Guamán Poma de Ayala. In the drawing *left* can be seen (top left) *Inti* the Sun and *raymi* the festival of the Sun celebrated in Cuzco in June. Top right: Coya was the wife and sister of the reigning Inca, whose children inherited the throne. The name also described the sacred virgins, wives of the Sun. Here the moon is pictured as the divine sister-wife of the Sun, and Queen of Heaven. Bottom left: the morning star. The word *uillca* is a term of divine honour. These symbols indicate that the Inca claims the divine Sun as his father, the Moon as his mother and the Morning Star as his brother. Bottom right: this shows Tambotocco, Paccari-tambo and the 'idol' Huanacauri – which figure in the legendary origin of the Inca dynasty. The *centre* drawing shows (top left) the bird whose feathers are like bright flowers. Top right: the *chunta*, or hard chonta tree, and at its foot an *otoronco*. Bottom left: the pouch for coca. Bottom right: two amaru snakes with the royal *borla* (tassel) in their mouths.

Opposite right. The Inca capital and sacred city of Cuzco, the heart of the Inca empire and of the religion of the Sun with which the Inca monarchy was identified, was constructed of fine megalithic architecture. Two styles were used: in one the stone blocks were rectangularly shaped and in the other style they were polygonal. In both styles the huge stones were fitted together with such accuracy that it is said a knife-blade cannot be thrust between them. The impressive Inca building can still be seen in Cuzco streets, where it often serves as the foundation for later Spanish Colonial building.

tell it of Sinchi Roca, who is the second monarch in the usual version, and assign the credit for the trick to his mother. She spread the word that the Sun was about to send a ruler and then produced the boy Sinchi Roca from the mouth of a cave, dressed in resplendent garments. The gullible people thereupon accepted him as a heaven-sent ruler and he thus became the first Inca monarch. Montesinos assigned the story of the four brothers to the dynasty of the Piruas, which according to him preceded the Inca by many centuries, and used the 'Shining Mantle' myth to account for the origin of the Inca dynasty with Sinchi Roca.

The Children of the Sun

Garcilaso Inca de la Vega, the author of the following account, claims to have been taught the official Inca legends as a boy by his uncles, who belonged to the Inca aristocracy.

'Know then, cousin, that in centuries past all this part of the earth consisted of great mountains and brushwood and the people in those times lived like wild animals without religion or polity, without houses or cities. They did not sow or cultivate the earth or clothe their bodies, for they did not know how to work cotton or wool for garments. They lived in twos and threes as they chanced to come together in caves and hollows and crevices of the rocks. Like beasts they ate wild plants and roots, the fruits which were produced by the bushes without cultivation, and human flesh. They covered their bodies

with leaves and bark and skins of animals; others went naked. In a word they lived like wild animals and like the brutes they even had their women in common. . .

'Our Father the Sun, seeing men as I have described them, was moved to pity and sent from the sky to earth one of his sons and daughters to instruct them in the knowledge of Our Father the Sun, that they might adore him and have him as their God, and to give them laws and prescriptions whereby they might live as men in reason and comity, that they might dwell in houses and cities, learn how to till the earth, cultivate and harvest food-plants, domesticate animals and enjoy the fruits of the earth like ra-

tional beings and no longer like animals. With this injunction and mandate Our Father the Sun sent down his two children to Lake Titicaca, which is eighty leagues from Cuzco, and told them to pass where they would and wherever they stayed to eat or to sleep they should sink in the soil a rod of gold which he gave them. This rod, half a yard long and two fingers thick, was to serve as a sign, for where it sank in the earth with a single blow there they were to stop and found the sacred city of the Sun.'

He concluded his instructions as follows:

' "When you have reduced these peoples to our service, you shall

Above. Detail from Paracas Necropolis woven textile. The very complicated feline and snake motif seems to indicate a developed and mature iconographical tradition, and thus a long established cult with associated mythology and beliefs. Unfortunately neither oral nor written records throw light on the mythological background of this early culture.

Opposite. Stirrup jar surmounted by a modelled head of a monkey with its arms painted on the body of the pot below. Royal Scottish Museum, Edinburgh.

maintain them in reason and justice with devotion, clemency and tenderness, playing in all things the part of a loving father to his beloved children, modelling yourselves on me. For I look to the well-being of the

whole world, since I give men my light by which they see and warm themselves when they are cold and make their pastures and fields to grow, their trees to bear and their flocks to multiply. I bring rain and fair weather in their season and each day I traverse the whole surface of the earth in order that I may see the needs of the world to succour and provide for them as the supporter and protector of men. It is my will that you my children follow this my example, sent to the earth solely to teach and aid these men who live like beasts. And to that end I name and establish you lords and kings of all races whom you thus benefit with your instructions and good government."

'Having thus declared his will, Our Father the Sun took leave of his children. They set out from Titicaca and journeyed to the north and throughout the whole journey wherever they stopped they tried to sink the rod of gold. But nowhere would it bury itself in the soil. So they came to a small roadside inn seven or eight leagues south of Cuzco, which today goes by the name Paccari-tambo or Inn of the Dawn. The Inca gave it that name because he left this inn at dawn, and the villagers today are very proud of the name. From there he and his wife, our Queen, came to the valley of Cuzco, which at this time was wild and unpopulated highland.

'The first stop they made in this valley was on the height called Huanacauri, south of the city. There the bar of gold sank entirely into the earth at a single blow and was not

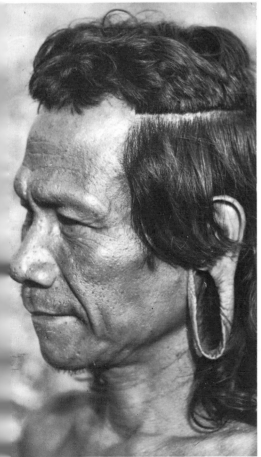

seen again. Thereupon our Inca said to his sister and wife:

' "It is in this valley that Our Father the Sun commanded us to make our abode in accordance with his will. Therefore, Queen and sister, it behoves each of us to go his way and draw the people to him in order to instruct them and care for them as Our Father the Sun enjoined." From the height of Huanacauri went forth our first monarchs, each in his own way, to gather together the peoples. And for this reason, since it was from there they sailed abroad to care for the well-being of mankind, we have erected there, as is common knowledge, a temple to the Sun in memory and honour of his beneficence to the world of men. The prince went towards the north and the princess to the south. To all the men and women they came upon in those barren regions they told how their Father the Sun had sent them from the sky to be lords and benefactors to the inhabitants of that land, removing them from the life of brutes which they had led and teaching them to live like men in towns and villages, eating the victuals of men. In this fashion our Kings spoke to the first savages they found in the mountain plateaus, and the latter, seeing these two persons clothed and adorned with the ornaments

Above. Hammered gold plaque from the Mochica culture. While Mochica pottery was naturalistic, the drawing and design followed the formalistic and symbolic tradition initiated by the Chavín culture. This design appears to represent two ritualistic figures with bird or animal masks, surmounted by animal headdresses, and carrying a dance staff topped by a human head whose square features are reminiscent of the carved stone head of Chavín. The figure on the right has a girdle terminating in a snake's head.

Above left. Ollantaytambo, an Inca pueblo and fortress in the Urubamba valley guarding the approaches to Machu Picchu. This is one of the most impressive examples of Inca building, a magnificent structure of stone terracing.

Below left. A Karaja Indian of Brazil. The enlarged earlobes usually hold large flat ornaments. The Inca nobility of times past also wore them, fashioned of gold and precious stones, and this led to their being dubbed *orejones* (long ears) by the Spaniards.

Opposite. Machu Picchu, the Lost City of the Inca, which was rediscovered by Hiram Bingham in 1912. It lies at the end of the gorge of the Urubamba river, on the edge of the tropical rain-forest. Behind it towers the peak of Huayna Picchu, flanked by precipices which rise 2,500 feet from the rapids. There are more than a hundred stairways in the ruins, the most imposing being that which leads from the central Plaza to the top of the hill on the left, on which still stands the *Intihuatana* or 'hitching post of the Sun'. The illustration shows stepped terraces leading up to the platform.

which Our Father the Sun had bestowed upon them, with their ears pierced and the lobes drawn low as is the fashion with us their descendants, and seeing that in their words and demeanour they showed themselves to be children of the Sun, marvelling at what they saw and won over by the promises made to them, they believed them in all things, according them reverence and worship as children of the Sun and obedience as Kings. Thus the word passed from one to another until large multitudes assembled ready to follow where our Kings might lead.

'Seeing the large numbers who flocked to their banner, our chiefs ordered some to gather food of the fields lest hunger should disperse them again and instructed others to make cottages and houses according to the model they supplied. In this fashion began to be built our imperial city, divided into two halves which they called Hanan Cuzco (which means upper Cuzco) and Hurin Cuzco (which is lower Cuzco). . .

'Meanwhile, as the city grew up, our Inca taught the male Indians the duties pertaining to the male, how to break and cultivate the soil, to sow the crops and grain and vegetables which he showed them were good for food. For this he taught them how to make ploughs and other necessary tools, instructed them in the manner of digging irrigation channels from the streams which water this valley of Cuzco, and even taught them to make the type of footgear we wear. The Queen on her part instructed the females in womanly offices, sewing and weaving cotton and wool, making garments for themselves and for their husbands and children. In a word there is nothing belonging to civilised life which our first chiefs omitted to teach their vassals, the Inca making himself instructor of the men and the Queen Coya instructress of the women. . .

'How many years ago the Sun Our Father sent these his first children I cannot tell you exactly. It was so long ago that it was not possible to retain the memory: we believe it was more than four hundred years. Our Inca was called Manco Capac and our Mama Coya was called Ocllo Huaco.

Opposite. The *Intihuatana* at Machu Picchu. These curiously cut stones of enormous size have been found set up on the summit of several Inca fortresses. They appear to be connected with calendrical calculations and so perhaps indirectly to have had significance in the cult of the sun-god. The *Intihuatana* may have been what the chronicler Montesinos referred to when he said of the Inca Capac Raymi Amauta that he 'called a great assembly of his wise men and astrologers and, with the king himself (who was deeply learned), they all studied the solstices with care. There was a sort of shadow-clock by which they knew which days were long and which were short, and when the sun went to and returned from the tropics.' Owing to the importance of the *Intihuatana* in Inca religion, the Spanish conquerors used to break off the stone wherever they found one. But Machu Picchu was never discovered by the Spanish and the *Intihuatana* is intact.

Below. A pair of ear ornaments from the Mochica culture. The mosaic design is contained in gold. A liking for large ear ornaments seems to be a feature of the South American Indian character. They are represented in all the pre-colombian cultures, and are much worn by the primitive tribes of today. American Museum of Natural History, New York.

As I have told you, they were brother and sister, children of the Sun and the Moon, our ancestors.' Garcilaso Inca de la Vega: *Comentarios Reales de los Incas*. Book I, Ch. 15.

The Shining Mantle

'Because of its distance in time the beginning of the Inca cannot be surely known except that they would tell in fable that from a cave or window in a certain building near Cuzco which they call Tambotocco or Paccari-tambo there came forth eight Inca brethren (others say only six, but the more general and plausible view is eight). The four males were thus called: the eldest Huana Cauri, the second Cusco Huanca, the third Manco Capac and the fourth Topa Ayar Cachi. The sisters were thus called: the eldest Topa Huaco, the second Mama Coya, the third Cori Ocllo, the fourth Ipa Huaco. These eight came forth to adventure together in search of lands which they could populate and before arriving at Cuzco they stopped at a place called Apitay, which some call Huana Cauri. The third sister, Cori Ocllo, being considered the most intelligent by the rest, went ahead in search of territory suitable for their purpose. And coming to the hutments of this city of Cuzco, which at that time was occupied by low and poor tribes of Indians called Lares, Poques and Huallas, before she arrived there she came upon a Poque Indian and slew him with a weapon called *macana*. She then cut him open and took out the lungs and blew them up and with these all bloody in her mouth she entered the town. Terrified at the sight, thinking that she fed on human flesh, the Indians abandoned their houses and fled. Judging the place to be good for settlement and that the natives were tame, she returned to where she had left her brethren and brought them there, except the eldest brother who wished to remain in Apitay, where he died. And they named the hill Huanacauri in his memory. The others occupied Cuzco without resistance and named the second brother, Cusco Huanca, chief of the city, for which reason the settlement was

called Cuzco, being named before that Acamama. He died in Coricancha and was succeeded by the third brother, called the great Manco Capac.

'This valiant Inca Manco Capac held sway over all that city of Cuzco, although he conquered no new territories. Yet some tell of these ancient Indians that there came from the great Lake Titicaca, which is in the province of Collao, to the said cave of Paccari-tambo certain brothers and sisters, called Cusco Huanca and Huana Cauri, noble and valiant persons and very warlike, who had their ears pierced and pieces of gold in the holes. The great Manco Capac was one of them and they say that he had beaten out two thin plaques of silver, placing one on his chest and the other on his back, and on his head he wore the diadem which they call *canipo*. He sent a certain Indian to the city with the message that he was the son of the Sun and he went to the top of a high peak where he showed himself walking to and fro with the silver plaques gleaming and flashing in the sun. When they saw this the Indians accepted him for the son of the Sun and a divine being and gave him

much riches and all that he wished for. Thus he became rich and powerful and sallied forth to conquer peoples in the neighbourhood of that city. . . Afterwards they say this great Manco Capac was changed into a stone which they greatly venerate.' Fray Martín de Morúa: *Historia del origen y genealogía real de los reyes Incas del Perú*. Chs. 2 and 3.

The Island of Titicaca

This account by Garcilaso illustrates how the Inca incorporated elements of Tiahuanaco myth in their own legends.

'Among other famous temples to the Sun which existed in Peru and which in the richness of the ornament of gold and silver could rival the temple of Cuzco, there was one in the island called Titicaca. It is in the lake of the same name rather more than two crossbow shots distant from the mainland, and five to six thousand paces in circumference. It is in this island that the Inca say the Sun set down his two children, male and female, when he sent them to earth to instruct in the arts of civilised life the barbarous peoples who up to then inhabited that land. With this fable they

Above. A brightly decorated poncho from the region of Lake Titicaca. Inca period. Musée de l'Homme, Paris.

Opposite. The shores of Lake Titicaca, at 12,500 feet above sea level the highest navigable lake in the world, stretching between Peru and Bolivia. The lake is 138 miles long and 70 miles across at its widest (222 km x 112.6 km), and its waters, of exceptional diaphaneity, reflect the intense blue of the sky with extraordinary depth and purity. Its serene beauty in the midst of the parched dreariness of the Altiplano has won it an almost mystical significance in the eyes of the Indians, and a mass of myth and legend centres on it. In the foreground of the picture is the curious rock structure popularly known as the *Horca de los Inca*, the 'Inca Gallows'.

Right. A bound mummy discovered in a burial tower in the region of Lake Titicaca. Museé de l'Homme, Paris.

join another from centuries earlier. They say that after the flood the rays of the sun appeared in that island and that great lake before they were seen in any other part. . . Seeing that the Indians believed this ancient fable and regarded the island and the lake as a sacred place, the first Inca, Manco Capac, in his natural ingenuity and sagacity took advantage of it and composed the second fable, saying that he and his wife were children of the Sun and that their father had set them down in that island so that they could go out from there all over the earth teaching the people, as has already been recorded. The Inca *amautas* – who were the philosophers and wise men of that kingdom – reduced the first fable to the second, treating it as a prophecy or prognostication. They said that the fact that the Sun cast his first rays on that island to illuminate the world had

been a sign and promise that there he would send down his first two children to teach and enlighten these peoples, freeing them from the bestialities in which they lived — as in fact the Inca monarchs did. With these and other similar inventions the Inca caused the Indians to believe that they were the children of the Sun and they confirmed the belief with the many benefits they conferred.

'Because of these two fables the Inca and all the people of their empire held that island for a holy place and so they ordered a splendidly rich temple to be built there and dedicated to the Sun. It was all lined with plaques of gold and all the provinces subject to the Inca offered there every year much gold and silver and precious stones in thanksgiving to the Sun for the two benefices which he had vouchsafed in that place. That temple had the same service as the temple at Cuzco. So much gold and silver from the offerings was heaped up on the island, in addition to what was fashioned for the temple service, that what the Indians say about it causes more astonishment than belief. Father Blas Valera, speaking of the wealth of that temple and the great surplus which was heaped up outside it, says that the transplanted Indians (called

---

Opposite. Reed boats on Lake Titicaca. These boats have been used for lake transport by the Indians of the highlands from time immemorial. Constructed from bundles of the totora reeds which grow beside the lake, they are often fitted with masts to carry a sail. The reeds were also used for making hawsers, bridges and so forth.

Right. The most common form of Mochica ceramic was the 'stirrup' vase in which a semicircular handle rises from the body of the vase and is surmounted by a single spout; they are first found in the Chavín horizon. Early Mochica stirrup vase in the form of a feline, perhaps a puma. The flat nose, prominent eyes and overlapping fangs are treated more naturalistically than in the Chavín style. The significance of the 'benedictory' gesture of the hands can only be conjectured, but the expression of the figure may well be benevolent rather than horrific. It may represent a priest or celebrant wearing a feline mask. Kemper Collection.

mitmac) living at Copacabana assured him that the surplus of silver and gold was such that another complete temple could have been made from it without the use of any other material. And they say that when the Indians learned of the entry of the Spaniards and that they came seizing any wealth they found, they threw it all into that great lake. . . *Comentarios Reales de los Incas.* Book III, Ch. 25.

What the Indians Report of their Beginning

'It is no matter of any great importance to know what the Indians themselves report of their beginning, being more like unto dreams than to true histories. They make great mention of a deluge which happened in their country. . . The Indians say that all men were drowned in the deluge, and they report that out of the great Lake Titicaca came one Viracocha, who stayed in Tiahuanaco, where at this day there is to be seen the ruins of ancient and very strange buildings, and from thence came to Cuzco, and so began mankind to multiply. They show in the same lake a small island, where they feign that the sun hid himself and so was preserved; and for this reason they make great sacrifices unto him in that place, both of sheep [i.e. llamas] and men.

'Others report that six, or I know not what number of men, came out of a certain cave by a window, by whom men first began to multiply; and for this reason they call them Paccari-tambo. And therefore they are of opinion that the Tambos are the most ancient race of men. They say also that Manco Capac, whom they acknowledge for the founder and chief of their Incas, was issued of that race and that from him sprang two families or lineages, the one of Hanan Cuzco and the other of Urin Cuzco. They say moreover that when the King Incas attempted war and conquered sundry provinces they gave a colour and made a pretext of their enterprise, saying that all the world ought to acknowledge them for that all the world was renewed by their race and country; and also that the

true religion had been revealed to them from heaven. But what availeth it to speak more, seeing that all is full of lies and vanity, far from reason?' Father José de Acosta: *The Natural and Moral History of the Indies.* Book I, Ch. 25 English translation by Edward Grimston, 1604.

The Origin of Nations and Cults

'And as to the origin of their idolatries it is thus that these peoples had no usage of writing but in a house of the Sun called Poquen Cancha, which is hard by Cuzco, they possessed paintings done on boards of the life of each one of the Incas and the lands he had conquered and also their origin. And among these paintings the following fable was also depicted.

'In the life of Manco Capac, who was the first Inca and from whom they began to boast themselves children of the Sun and from whom they derived their idolatrous worship of the Sun, they had an ample account of the deluge. They say that in it perished all races of men and created things insomuch that the waters rose above the highest mountain peaks in the world. So it was that no living thing remained except one man and

Left. Roughly carved, primitive figure of a man from Chavín. The straight flat nose later became conventional. Although this highly individual art style is conventionalised and sophisticated, the effect is massive and strong – often expressive and urgent.

Opposite. Religious practices and huacas of the peoples of the Inca Empire.
   Opposite above left. Tupa Inca. The Inca speaks with all the *huacas.* 'Sacred Huacas: may one of you deities enjoin that there shall not be rain nor snow-storm nor hail. I the Inca say this only.' Enclosed by the circle of *huacas* are the words in Quechua: 'They are not like us, the Inca.' The figure on top of the mountain peak Huanacauri represents Ayar Uchu, brother of the Inca Manco Capac, who according to the legend was changed to stone.
   Opposite below left. Indians of the western part of the empire, according to Guamán Poma de Ayala, had their own idols and *huacas* whom they honoured as well as those of the official Inca religion. They sacrificed gold and silver, coca, the fruit of the molle tree, flamingo feathers, twelve-year-old children, and black llama-kids. Here they bring offerings to the *huaca* Cocopona.
   Opposite above right. The Indians of the Collao sacrifice a black llama and coca to the spirit of Villcanota. This drawing by Guamán Poma de Ayala reflects what he knew of the religious practices of the region in Inca times. The true Tiahuanaco period pre-dates this, however, and was probably suppressed by the Incas.
   Opposite below right. A family of Indians worshipping Pachacamac, see p 105. The cult of this creator god pre-dated the Inca supremacy, but was maintained by them alongside their cult of the sun. The temple of Pachacamac was in a valley south of the present city of Lima, and was a centre of pilgrimage. Devotion to this god persisted and he was later identified by the Indians with the Christian god. Drawing by Guamán Poma de Ayala.

On page 50-51. Pectoral or head ornament from Esmeraldas, Ecuador, in hammered gold depicting a bat deity flanked by four human figures. University Museum, Philadelphia, Pennsylvania.

one woman. And what time the waters subsided the wind cast them up at Tiahuanaco, which will be more than seventy leagues from Cuzco, a little more or less. The creator of all things commanded them there to remain as *mitmacs* [colonists; persons transplanted and settled elsewhere than in the place of their birth.] And there in Tiahuanaco the Creator began to make the peoples and tribes who are in the land, fashioning of clay one of each nation and painting the garments which each was to wear and keep to. Those that were to go with long hair he painted with long hair and those that were to wear it short with short. This done, he gave to each nation the language it was to speak and the songs they were to sing and the seeds and foodstuffs they were to grow.

'When he had finished painting and creating the said nations and lumps of clay he gave being and soul to each one as well the men and the women and commanded each nation to sink below the earth. Thence each nation passed underground and came up in the places to which he assigned them. Thus they say that some came out of caves, others from hills, others out of fountains, others from lakes, others from tree boles and other rubbish of this kind. They say that because they issued forth from these places and began to multiply, and had the beginning of their lineage from them, they made *huacas* and places of worship of them in memory of the beginning of their lineage which proceeded out from them. Thus every nation of people uses the dress with which they clothe their *huaca.* And they say that

CAPITVLO DE LOS IDOLOS
VACA BILLCA INCAP

IDOLOS IVACAS.
DELOS CCLLASVIOS

IDOLOS IVACAS
DELOS CONDESVIOS

IDOLOS IVACAS
DELOS CHINCHAISV ivs

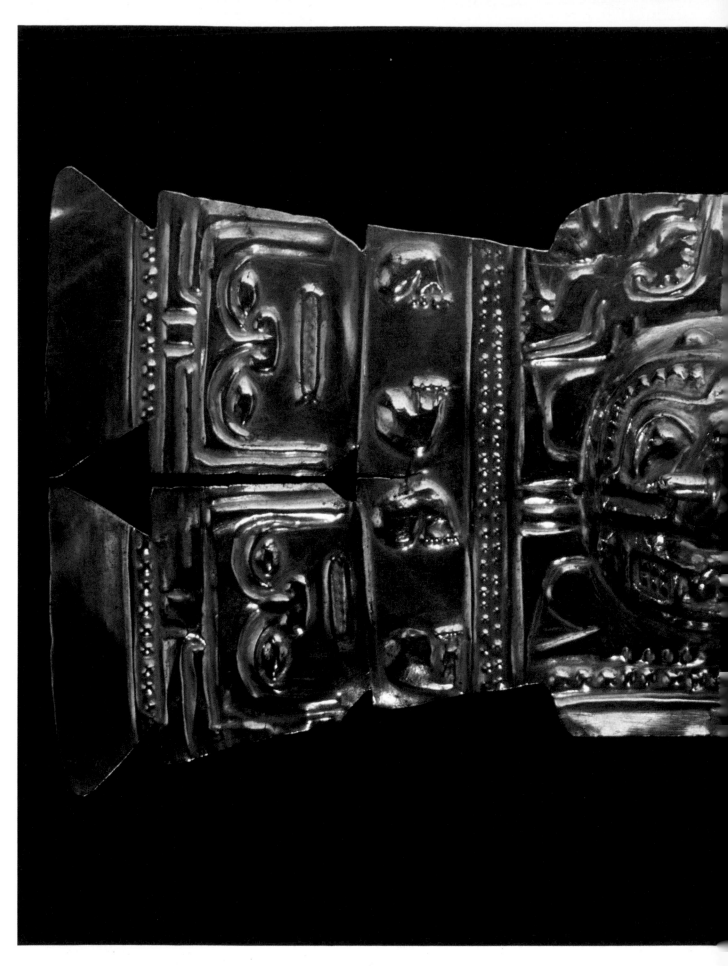

Left. A ceremonial knife, fashioned in gold and originally inlaid with turquoise, from the Lambayeque Valley where a seaborne hero called Naymlap is said to have founded a kingdom in the twelfth century. It was once believed that the figure portrayed was of Naymlap himself but this is now regarded as unlikely since this decorative theme also appears in the art of the other coastal cultures. Museum für Volkerkunde, Berlin.

Opposite. Religious practices and huacas of the peoples of the Inca Empire.
Opposite above left. According to Guamán Poma the Indians of the Antisuyu – the eastern part of the Inca Empire, which included the tropical forest area – buried their dead in hollow trees.
Opposite above right. The Indians of the Kuntisuyu – the eastern part of the empire – dressed their dead in rich garments and walled them up in stone sepulchres.
Opposite below left. Guamán Poma describes the ceremony of the dead, which took place in November. The dead were taken from their tombs, offered food and drink, dressed in rich garments with feathers on their heads and carried through the streets with singing and dancing.
Opposite below right. Guamán Poma describes the superstition of the sorcerers. He here pictures, in the form of Christian devils, the devil who visits a person in sleep, the devil of fire and the devil who sucks the spirit from a man.

the first to be born from that place returned there and were turned into stones, or others into falcons and condors and other animals and birds. Thus the *huacas* they use and worship are of different form.'

'There are other peoples who say that when the deluge was ended mankind was destroyed by the waters except those – and they were very few – who had been able to escape on hills on in caves or trees and that from them they began to multiply. And in memory of those first progenitors who had escaped in these places they made idols of stone and to each *huaca* they gave the name of him from whom they claimed their race was descended. Thus they worshipped and made sacrifice of such articles as each tribe used. Yet there were some tribes who retained a tradition even

ENTIERO DE ANTISVIOS

mitaca arbol

yquima

aya

enticrro · · · como

ENTIERO DE LOS CONDESVIOS

amoyanacen utapnaca

conquirmana mallco

enticrro · · · como

NOBIENBRE AIA MARCAI

quilla

la fiesta delos defuntos

aya

HICHEZEROS DE 3VEÑOS LIVII Aı AICA VMV

hichezero de sueño

hichezero de fuego

hichezero q chupa

53

before they were subjected by the Inca of a Creator of all things, and although they made sacrifices to him it was not in such quantity or with such reverence as they sacrificed to their *huacas*.

'But to return to our myth. They say that the Creator was in Tiahuanaco and that was his principle abode. Hence there are there superb edifices deserving of wonder in which are painted many dresses of those Indians and many stone figures of men and women whom he turned into stone for not obeying his commands. They say that over all was the darkness of

Left. Carved stone figure from Chavín de Huántar. The broad flat nose and enlarged eyes have some resemblance to the early sculptures figures found at Tiahuanaco, although the face lacks the high cheek bones of the Tiahuanaco figures. The engraved decoration is less stylised than most of the Chavín carving which has come down to us.

Opposite. Gold breastplate from Lambayeque, modelled in characteristic style of Chavín de Huántar combining feline features and snake heads. Cleveland Museum of Art, Ohio. Purchase, Dudley F. Allen Fund.

Below. Gold eagle pectoral from the Popayán region, Colombia. Height 3.75 inches (9.5 cm).

night and there he created the Sun and the Moon and stars and that he commanded the Sun, the Moon and the stars to go to the island of Titicaca which is near by and from there to ascend to the sky.

'And at the moment when the Sun was about to ascend in the form of a man all shining and resplendent, he called to the Incas and to Manco Capac and said: "Thou and thy descendants are to be lords and subdue many nations. Regard me as thy father and yourselves as my children and reverence me as thy father." Having said these words he gave to Manco Capac as his insignia and arms the *suntur paucar* and the *champi* [royal Inca headdress and mace] and the other insignia which they used in the manner of a sceptre. At that point he commanded the Sun, the Moon and the stars to ascend to the sky and take their proper places there; and they did so. And at the same moment Manco Capac and his brothers and sisters, at the command of the Creator, sank beneath the earth and came out at the cave of Paccari-tambo, which they regard as their place of origin, although it is said that other races also came out of the said cave at the point where the Sun rose on the first day after the Creator had divided night from day. From this they obtained the name children of the Sun and worshipped and reverenced the Sun as their father.

'The Indians also have another myth in which they say that the Creator had two sons, one of whom they called Imaymana Viracocha and the other Tocapo Viracocha. When the Creator had fashioned the peoples and nations, giving to each their appropriate appearance and language, and had sent the Sun, Moon and stars to their places in the

sky from Tiahuanaco, as has been said, the Creator, whom the Indians in their own language call Pachaya-chachic [Teacher of the World] or Ticci Viracocha, which means the Unknowable God, went along the highland road and visited the tribes to see how they had begun to multiply and to fulfil the commandments he had given them. Finding that some tribes had rebelled against his commands, he changed a large part of them into stones in the shape of men and women with the same costume that they had worn.

'The changing into stone occurred at the following places: in Tiahuanaco, in Pucara and Jauja, where they say he turned the *huaca* called Huarivilca into stone, and in Pachacamac, in Cajamarca and other regions. Indeed today there are huge figures of stone in these places, some of them almost the size of giants, which must have been fashioned by human hands in times of great antiquity and as the memory failed and in the absence of writing they invented this legend saying that the people were turned into stones by command of the Creator on account of disobeying his commands.

'They also say that at Pucara, which is forty leagues from Cuzco on the Collao road, fire came down from heaven and burnt a great part of them while those who tried to escape were turned into stone. The Creator, who they say was the father of Imaymana Viracocha and Tocapo Viracocha, commanded Imaymana Viracocha, the elder of his two sons, in whose power all things are placed, to set out from that place and traverse all the world by the road of the mountains and forested valleys. As he went he was to give names to all the trees large and small, to the flowers and fruit they were to bear, and to indicate to

Above. A Chimu figurine in gold, possibly a votive offering. The headdress suggests a priest, who carries a maize plant and a spade. Maize was the staff of life of the high civilisations of Peru.

Opposite. A figure of a water-carrier in gold from the Inca period.

56

the people which were edible and which not and which had medicinal properties. He also gave names to the herbs and flowers, and the time when they were to produce flowers and fruits and taught people which could cure and which would kill. His other son named Tocapo Viracocha, which in their language means "the Maker", he ordered to go by the road of the plains, visiting the peoples and giving names to the rivers and trees and instructing them as to the fruits and flowers. And thus they went to the lowest parts of this land until they came to the sea, where they ascended into the sky after having finished making all that there is in the land.

'In the same myth they also say that at Tiahuanaco, where he created the tribes of men, he created all the different kinds of birds, male and female of each, giving them the songs which each kind was to sing. Those that were to inhabit the forests he sent to the forests and those which were to inhabit the highlands to the highlands, each to the region proper to its kind. He also created all the different species of animals, male and female of each, and all the snakes and creeping things there are in the land and commanded each to its proper habitat. And he taught the people the names and properties of the birds and snakes and other reptiles.

'These Indians also believed that neither the Creator nor his sons were born of woman and that they were unchanging and eternal. The various tribes of this country have many other nonsensical beliefs and fables about their origin insomuch that if we were to record them all, it would be very prolix and there would be no end to it.' Cristóbal de Molina of Cuzco: *The Fables and Rites of the Yncas.*

Mythology of the Collao

Tiahuanaco

The village of Tiahuanaco, now a few miles from the shores of Lake Titicaca on the Bolivian Altiplano, or Collao, is the site of some of the most astonishing and enigmatic megalithic remains of South America. They were the centre of an important highland civilisation and religion, thought to have been later than the coastal culture of Chavín but earlier than the flourishing coastal kingdom of Chimu which preceded the Inca. The culture and the art styles of Tiahuanaco spread, perhaps by conquest, to the coastal regions of Peru and may have swamped the early coastal cultures of Mochica and Nazca. The collapse of Tiahuanaco was followed by a period of political anarchy and regional warring groups on the Altiplano until the area was conquered and unified by the Inca monarchs. The cause of the collapse is obscure. Almost everything to do with the Tiahuanaco civilisation has been a matter of conflicting theories among modern archaeologists and nothing can be regarded as certain.

By the time the first Spaniards visited the Bolivian Altiplano all detailed memory of the Tiahuanaco culture had passed from men's minds. The absence of recorded traditions is not due to incuriosity on the part of Spanish chroniclers, as it was in the case of the coastal kingdom of Chimu and Pachacamac near Lima. For the Spaniards were impressed by what they saw at Tiahuanaco – the most sensational archaeological remains of the continent – and at other localities in the neighbourhood of Lake Titicaca.

It is one of the mysteries of South American mythology and legend that, although they questioned the local Indians closely, no traditions from the period of Tiahuanaco ascendancy were available to them. The local Indians – who according to Cieza de León and other chroniclers were by no means unintelligent – themselves regarded the unfinished ruins as a thing miraculous and foreign to them. They knew with complete assurance that they dated from a time far more ancient .than the Inca monarchy. But they did not know what people had been responsible for them – except only that it was not their own ancestors. They possessed a cycle of cosmological myth incorporating stories of a deluge, creation and a divine culture hero. They also retained legends of their past history which embodied memories of a hunting and food-gathering stage before the introduction of agriculture and handicrafts. But they had no traditions from the Tiahuanaco culture.

The evidence of archaeology points certainly to the existence of a very highly centralised social organisation, whether religious or political, which must have preceded the Inca regime and must have lasted many centuries on the Bolivian Altiplano with its centres at Tiahuanaco and other sites in the vicinity of Lake Titicaca. This must be assumed in order to account for the high level of megalithic technology, the stone carvings, the elaborately developed iconography, the exquisite handicrafts and the perfec-

Large Nazca jar with what may be a demon face and arm gripping a severed head. The vase is surrounded with modelled heads in three different colours. Whether this has a religious and mythological significance in connection with a sacrificial cult or whether it has rather a military significance can only be conjectured.

59

tion of a distinctive artistic style which spread from the highlands over much of the coastal area of Peru. The oblivion in which this great civilisation was submerged is the more astonishing in a people generally notable for the length and retentiveness of their racial memories.

Two theories have been advanced to account for the loss of this tradition. One supposes that the people who built up the Tiahuanaco civilisation were overthrown by warlike immigrants, who wiped them out and liquidated their culture and traditions. The other theory suggests that, in accordance with the policy of moving populations, when the Inca sovereigns conquered the Collao, they

transplanted the local peoples and settled on the Altiplano other races who had no traditions about the Tiahuanaco past. Both these theories are necessarily speculative.

Three facts tell slightly in favour of the former. First, the building at Tiahuanaco was left unfinished and seems to have stopped abruptly. There are still partly worked stones at the site and one may still see roughly fashioned stones of great size left lying at the quarries from which they came. The second is the legend that during a time of disturbance and anarchy (apparently between the fall of Tiahuanaco and the dominance of the Inca), two chieftains, Cari and Zapana, rose up and made war on

each other; and that as a result of this the then Inca king was able to obtain easy control. This story would seem to indicate the existence of some historical memories from before the Inca conquest, though without any traditions from the time of Tiahuanaco greatness. The third fact, for what it is worth, is a curious legend of an early race of 'white and bearded' people in the region of Titicaca, who were entirely destroyed as a result of a war with a later arriving people and disappeared without leaving any trace of their existence. The recurrent story of a 'white and bearded' race (the peoples of South America are of various shades of bronze and lacking in facial hair) is no doubt best regarded

as an indication that the mythopoeic fancy was still active at the time of the Spanish Conquest; existing legends of an earlier race who were conquered and liquidated in the distant past by the present inhabitants might well have been conflated with stories which were circulated of the new and terrifying white arrivals.

The Accounts of the Spanish Chroniclers

'Although the temple of Tiahuanaco was a universal shrine and *huaca*,

Above. The rim of a shallow plate of the Mochica culture from Chimbote. Soldiers are seen tormenting their prisoners, who are forced to run naked with halters round their necks, their noses mutilated. The desert location is plainly indicated by cactuses, etc., and the formalised design gives the whole the look of some sadistic rite.

Opposite. Double spouted vase in Black Chimu ware. The upper half of the body is decorated with conventionalised animal and human figures analogous in style and iconography to the relief decorations on the walls of Chanchan. On the bridge is the head of a deity or crowned king with prostrate worshipping figures. Kemper Collection.

. . . the Indians esteemed it chiefly on account of its size and antiquity, for indeed the buildings are the most magnificent and spectacular of any in this kingdom. . . The ruins are about two hundred paces to the south of the village. Its name before it came under the sway of the Incas was Paypicala, a word from the Aymará which is the language of the natives of that district and which means "the stone in the middle". For the Indians of the Collao believe that that village was at the middle of the world and that from

Stone jar in the shape of a puma, carved with characteristic patterns in the style of Chavín de Huantar. University Museum, Philadelphia, Pennsylvania.

it set forth the men who were to re-populate the world after the deluge. It got the name Tiahuanaco for the following reason. The locals say that, when an Inca king happened to be there, there arrived from Cuzco a runner; and when the Inca learned the extraordinary speed with which he had run the distance he said to him: "Tiay huanacu", which in the Inca tongue means: "Sit down and rest, guanaco". [A guanaco is an animal of the alpaca family.] He called him this because the guanaco is the speediest animal of the country, and this sentence became the name of the village...

'I find two things worthy of especial note in connection with these edifices: the first is the astonishing size of the stones and the whole work and the second their great antiquity... The principal cause for the great veneration in which the Indians hold this shrine must have been its great antiquity. The natives have considered it sacred from time immemorial before they were conquered by the kings of Cuzco, as also did those kings after they became lords of this province. The latter made Pumapuncu a famous temple, ennobling it and enriching it, increasing its adornment and the number of priests and sacrifices. And near to it they built the Royal Palaces in which they say Manco Capac was born, the son of Huayna Capac, and their ruins can be seen today. It was a very large edifice with many rooms and compartments.

'The rumour that great abundance of riches was buried in these buildings has induced some Spaniards to excavate them in search of it and they have found at various times many pieces of gold and silver, though not as much as was thought to be there. And in truth this greed to possess the treasures which common belief supposes to be hidden there has been a chief cause for the destruction and spoiling of this structure. They have also despoiled it in order to make use

Above. Mochica stirrup vase with a human-headed crab on a platform. The face shows great character despite the bulging eyes and prominent jaguar fangs. It wears a high headdress and snake or feline ear pendants. Some historians presume that this represents a 'crab-deity' but we have no evidence for deity or ritual apart from the representations. Kemper Collection.

Above right. Seated figure from Pokótia at the foot of the mountain ridge of Quimzachata south of Tiahuanaco. It is now in the open-air Tiahuanaco museum of La Paz. It belongs to the earlier of the two periods of sculpture found at Tiahuanaco, which produced impressive over life-size heads and kneeling figures. The faces are not Aymara in type, but memory of the people who made them is lost. Spanish chronicles say the native populace connected them with local creation mythology, with belief in an earlier race of giants and a race of men turned into stone by the creator.

Right. 'Devil' mask worn by a participant in a Corpus Christi procession; it incorporates the jaguar fangs which were a feature of Peruvian iconography from the earliest Chavín times and is surmounted by a headdress embroidered with a Sun symbol. In the processions for such Christian festivals the traditional costumes and masks are often worn by those following the Cross and other Christian symbols. Among the highland Indians of the Altiplano the ancient religions, superstitions and ritual customs persist in synthesis with the Catholic Christianity brought by the Spaniards.

of the stones. For the church of Tiahuanaco was built from them and the inhabitants of the town of Chuquiago [La Paz] carried off many to build their houses, and even the Indians in the village of Tiahuanaco make their tombs from beautiful stone tiles which they obtain from the ruins. . .' Padre Bernabé Cobo: *Historia del Nuevo Mundo.*

'It is my belief that these ruins are the most ancient of all Peru and the general opinion is that some of these edifices were made a long time before the reign of the Inca. Indeed I have heard it stated by the Indians that the Inca constructed the great buildings of Cuzco on the model of the wall which can be seen here. More, they say that the first Incas were in two minds whether to make the seat of

their empire at Tiahuanaco. . . I asked the natives in the presence of Juan Vargas (who has the *encomienda* over them) whether these edifices were built in the time of the Inca and they laughed at the question, affirming that they were made long before the Inca reign but they could not say who had made them, only that they had heard from their forbears that everything to be seen there appeared suddenly in the course of a single night. From this, and from the fact that they also say bearded men had been seen in the island of Titicaca and that similar people had made the edifice at Vinaque, I would say that perhaps it may have been that before the Inca rule a civilised and intelligent people may have immigrated to this region, though where they came from is not known, but being few, and the native

Above. Monolithic gateway at Tiahuanaco, known locally as the Gateway of the Sun. The elaborately carved frieze with large central figure and rows of subsidiary figures in highly conventionalised relief is typical of the Tiahuanacan art style and iconography. The megalithic ruins and the surviving statuary are the most imposing archaeological remains of South America. With the expansion of the highland power, whether by conquest or by trade, the style and iconographic motifs spread northwards into Peru and influenced much of the coastal area, where it is known as 'coastal Tiahuanaco'.

population so numerous, they may have been wiped out in the wars.' Pedro de Cieza de León: *Crónica del Perú* Part I, Ch. 105.

Origin Myths of the Collao
'Many of these Indians [i.e. of the Collao] tell that they have heard from their ancestors that in times past there

Opposite. Detail of the Gateway of the Sun, showing the central figure and the subordinate running figures, all carrying sceptres or staffs of office, topped by what are perhaps formalised condor heads. The meaning of the figures and the symbols has been lost, for the memory of the Tiahuanacan people and their empire was systematically overlaid with the official Inca legend and the remains were already a matter of mystery and astonishment to the local Indians when the site was first visited by Spanish Conquistadores. We know, at least, that the site was connected with the origin myths of the highland Indians; and the powerful central figure may represent their supreme creator-deity before the Inca cult of the Sun was introduced to the Collao.

Below. Cast copper plaque representing in highly stylised form a human figure between two felines. Above are two conventionalised figures which may represent a fox or ant-eater motif. Aguada culture of the north-west Argentine, A.D. 700–1000. University Museum of Archaeology and Ethnology, Cambridge.

Left. Monolithic figure now set up on the Kalasasaya, or Temple of the Sun, at Tiahuanaco. It is known locally as El Fraile, "the Friar". Posnansky nevertheless believed that it represented a female figure, perhaps dedicated to lacustrine worship since the decorations engraved upon it appear to be connected with the fauna of the lake. The waist band, for example, is carved with stylised crustaceans which may be the *hyalela* found in Lake Titicaca. The right hand holds a sceptre and the left carried an object which may be a ceremonial *keru*. Carved from a single block of red sandstone, the statue is over six feet high.

Opposite above. Two of the high masonry towers, *chullpas*, thought to be burial towers which are found in Bolivia and around Lake Titicaca. They date from the period about A.D. 1000 and after, when the power of Tiahuanaco had been broken but the Inca ascendancy not yet established. The admirable masonry and structure suggest that, while the strength of the state had gone, the skill of the Tiahuanaco artisans had survived.

Opposite below. Pottery beaker from Tiahuanaco. The relief design of a conventionalised human figure seems to belong in style to a somewhat earlier period than the classical style illustrated by the iconography of the Gate of the Sun. It is not known whether the figure represents a deity or a priest-king. Kemper Collection.

was a great deluge . . . and give it to be understood that their ancestors are of great antiquity, and they relate so many stories and fables about their origin that I shan't stop to write them down. For some say that their ances-tors came forth from a fountain, some from a rock, some from a lake, so that it is impossible to get anything else from them about their origins. But they all agree that their forbears lived in a state of anarchy before the Inca held sway over them. Their strongholds were high in the mountains and from there they made war and their manners were corrupt. Later they learned from the Incas everything that their other subjects were taught and they began to build their villages in the same manner as now. . .

'Before the Incas reigned over them many of these Indians of the Collao say that there were two great lords in their province, one called Zapana and the other Cari, and that these conquered many *pucaras*, which are their fortresses. And one of them entered the larger of the two islands in Lake Titicaca and found there a race of white people with beards and fought with them until he had killed them all. And after that they say there were heavy battles against the Canas and Canchas. And after they had done notable exploits these two lords who had arisen in the Collao turned their arms against each other. They sought the support of the Inca Viracocha, who then reigned at Cuzco, and he made an alliance with Cari at Chucuito and displayed such adroitness that he made himself master over many peoples of the Collao without fighting. . .

'These natives of the Collao say the same as all the highland peoples that the Creator of all things is called Ticci Viracocha and they know that his principal abode is in heaven. But deceived by the Devil, they adored various other gods, as all the heathen did. They have a kind of romances or songs by means of which the memory of events is preserved and they do not forget it in spite of the lack of writing. And among the natives of this Collao are men of good understanding who show their intelligence when they are questioned. They keep count of time and know something of the movements both of the sun and the moon. . .' Cieza de León. Part I, Ch. 100.

'I often asked the natives of these regions what they knew about their condition before they were subjected by the Inca. They say that men lived in those times in a state of disorder, many went naked like savages; they had no houses or other dwellings than caves (many of which can be seen high in the mountains) and from these they went forth to gather whatever they could find to eat in the countryside. Some made fortresses, called *pucara*, in the highlands and they sallied forth from these to fight one another. Many were killed and they carried off the spoils and women of the conquered. They were in a state of anarchy without political cohesion and had no overlords but only petty chiefs who led them in battle. Their clothing was primitive, but they say that the headbands or *llautu* by which one tribe is nowadays distinguished from another were used even then.

'When they were living in this state

there rose up in the province of the Collao a powerful chief named Zapana, who brought many people under his command. One other thing they say, but whether it is true or not only the Almighty God knows who understands all things; as for me, my only authority is the testimony of the Indians. They assert with assurance that after this great captain arose in Hatun Colla there appeared in the district of the Canas, which is between the Canchas and Collao, near the village of Chugara, women who were as valiant as men. These women took up arms and made themselves masters of the district, where they lived without husbands almost as it is told of the Amazons. After some years these people clashed with Zapana, who had made himself lord of Hatun Colla, and built walled fortresses, which still exist, to defend themselves against him. But after they had done all they could they were defeated and killed and their name died out...

'They also relate that long ago in the island of Titicaca there were people with beards like ourselves. And coming from the valley of Coquimbo, their captain, who was called Cari, came to the place where

Chucuito now stands, and after making a new settlement there crossed over to the island...

'Before the Incas ruled or had even been heard of in these kingdoms these Indians relate a thing more noteworthy than anything else they say. They assert that they were a long time without seeing the sun and, suffering much hardship from this, they offered prayers and vows to those whom they held for gods, beseeching of them the light they lacked. At this the sun very brilliant rose from the island of Titicaca in the great lake of the Collao, and all were rejoiced. After this had happened they say that there suddenly appeared, coming from the south, a white man of large stature and authoritative demeanour. This man had such great power that he changed the hills into valleys and from the valleys made great hills, causing streams to flow from the living stone. When they saw his power they called him Maker of all things created and Prince of all things, Father of the sun. For he did other still more wonderful things, giving being to men and animals; in a word by his hand very great benefits accrued to them. This is the story that the Indians themselves told me and

they heard it from their fathers who in their turn had it from the old songs which were handed down from very ancient times.

'They say that this man travelled along the highland route to the north, working marvels as he went and that they never saw him again. They say that in many places he gave men instructions how they should live, speaking to them with great love and kindness and admonishing them to be good and to do no damage or injury one to another, but to love one another and show charity to all. In most places they name him Ticci Viracocha, but in the province of Collao he is called Tuapaca [Thunupa] or in some parts of it Arunaua. In many places they built temples to him and in them they set up statues in his likeness and offered sacrifices before them. The huge statues in the village of Tiahuanaco are held to be from those times. Although they relate what I have recorded about Ticci Viracocha based on the tradition of past time, they can say no more about him nor whether he ever returned to any part of that kingdom.

'They relate further that after much time had passed they saw another man like in appearance to the first but they do not mention his name. They have it from their forbears that wherever he passed he healed all that were sick and restored sight to the blind by words alone. Thus he was beloved by all. So, working great miracles by his words, he came to the district of the Canas and there, near a village called Cacha ... the people rose up against him and threatened to stone him. They saw him sink to his knees and raise his hands to heaven as if beseeching aid in the peril which beset him. The Indians declare that thereupon they saw fire in the sky which seemed all around them. Full of fear, they approached him whom they had intended to kill and besought him to forgive them; for they regarded this as a punishment for their sin in seeking to stone a stranger. Presently they saw that the fire was extinguished at his command, though the stones were consumed by fire in such wise that large blocks could be lifted by hand as if they were cork. They narrate further that, leaving the place where this occurred, he came to the coast and there, holding his mantle, he went forth amidst the waves of the sea and was seen no more. And as he went they gave him the name Viracocha, which means "foam of the sea".' Cieza de León. Part II, Chs. 4 and 5.

Creation Myths of the Collao
'They say that in ancient times the land of Peru was dark and there was no light nor day in it. In those times there dwelt there a certain people who owed allegiance to an overlord whose name they no longer remember. And they say that in those times when all was night in the land there came forth from a lake in the district called Collasuyu, a Lord named Con Ticci Viracocha bringing with him a certain number of people, though they don't remember how many. And after emerging from the lake he went to a place nearby, where is now the village they call Tiahuanaco in the Collao. And while he was there with his followers they say that he suddenly made the sun and the day and commanded the sun to follow the course which it does follow. Then he made the stars and the moon. They say that this Con Ticci Viracocha had

Above. Stirrup jar modelled and painted in the form of a lobster. Museum of Mankind, London.

Opposite. Double-spouted Nazca vessel painted with fish, possibly sharks. Museum Rietberg, Zurich.

emerged on an earlier occasion and that on this first appearance he made the heaven and the earth and left everything dark. It was then that he created this race of men who lived during the times of darkness. And this race did something which angered Viracocha, so he came forth the second time as has been said and turned that race and their overlord to stone as a punishment for the anger they had caused him.

'So, as has been said, when he emerged he made the sun and day and moon and stars. This done, he made at Tiahuanaco stone models or patterns of the peoples he was afterwards

70

Above. Polished clay stirrup jar. The scene depicted is open to numerous interpretations but the most likely one is religious ritual. The priest(?) is grasped by a man or worshipper wearing a mask on his head. The beast represented is like no known animal of the Pacific coast; the central crest suggests that it was purely imaginary.

Opposite. Square-cut head, almost four feet high, belonging to the later period of Tiahuanaco sculptures, in which highly stylised gigantic figures were often covered with symbolic relief carving or engraved decoration. This head is now in the open-air museum of La Paz.

to produce, and he did it in the following way. He made from stone a certain number of people and a lord who governed them and many women who were pregnant and others who had young children in cradles after their custom. When this was done he set the stone figures apart and made another province there in Tiahuanaco also of stone in the same manner. When this was done he commanded all the people with him to journey forth, keeping only two with him, and these he commanded to look at the stone figures he had made and the names he had given them, saying to them: "These are called so and so and will issue forth from such and

such a fountain in such and such a province and shall increase and populate it; these others shall issue from such and such a cave and shall be named such and such and shall populate such and such a region. As I have them here painted and fashioned of stone, so shall they issue from fountains, rivers, caves and rocks in the provinces that I have indicated to you. And all you my people shall go in that direction (indicating the direction of sunrise), dividing them up and indicating the title each is to bear."

'Thus those viracochas went off to the various districts which Viracocha had indicated to them and as soon as each arrived in his district he called those stone figures which Viracocha had commanded in Tiahuanaco were to issue forth in that district, each viracocha taking up his position close by the site where he had been told they were to come forth. When this was done, the Viracocha at Tiahuanaco spoke in a loud voice: "So and so, come forth and people this land which is deserted, for thus has commanded Con Ticci Viracocha who made the world." There upon these peoples come forth from the places and regions which the Viracocha had instructed. Thus they went on calling

forth the races of men from caves, rivers and fountains and the high sierras and peopling the earth towards the east.

'And when Con Ticci Viracocha had accomplished this, then he sent forth the two who had remained behind with him in Tiahuanaco, to call forth the races of men in the same manner aforesaid. One he sent through the province of Cuntisuyu, that is to the left if one stands in Tiahuanaco with one's back to the sunrise, to bring forth the Indians native to the province of Cuntisuyu in the manner as aforesaid. The other he sent through the province of Antisuyu, which is on the right hand if one stands with the back to the sunrise.

'When he had despatched those two they say that he himself left towards Cuzco, which lies between those provinces, travelling by the royal road over the sierra in the direction of Cajamarca. As he went he called forth the races of men in the manner you have heard. When he came to the district called Cacha, the district of the Canas, eighteen leagues from the city of Cuzco, and when he called forth these Canas they came forth armed; and when they saw Viracocha, not knowing him, they rushed upon him weapons in hand, intending to kill him. Understanding their purpose, when he saw them coming thus upon him he suddenly made fire fall from heaven, burning a mountain peak in the direction where the Indians were. The Indians saw the fire, and were terrified of being burned, so they cast their weapons on the ground and fled straight towards Viracocha. When they reached him they all cast themselves on the ground. And when he saw them so, he took a staff in his hand, went to where the fire was and gave it two or three blows, whereupon it died out.

'Afterwards he told the Canas that he was their creator and they made a sumptuous *huaca* (that is, an idol or place of worship) in the place where it happened, and they and their descendants offered much gold and silver to the *huaca*. And in memory of this Viracocha and what happened they

73

Right. An unusually large vessel (20 inches/51 cm high, 10 inches/25.5 cm diameter) in painted terracotta of the Mochica culture. These figures, with the huge ear plugs and a mace in the right hand, are commonly called 'warriors' but they may equally represent noblemen or chieftains. Art Institute of Chicago, Illinois. Buckingham Fund.

Far right. An example of the pottery work found in the desolate Paracas peninsula, where nothing exists today but red sand. But buried under this lay the remains of a people unknown to history, undiscovered until 1925, who produced remarkable textiles and the mask shown here. The decoration is resin paint and was applied after firing. First century B.C. Dumbarton Oaks, Washington D.C. Robert Woods Bliss Collection.

Opposite. Early Nazca vase shaped in the form of a human figure with a foxskin headdress and stylised snake decorations. The figure wears what appears to be a necklace of silver plaques. Although we can only conjecture, it seems likely that these accoutrements indicate a ceremonial function in connection with local cult.

---

set up in the *huaca* a huge sculpted stone figure on a large stone base about five yards long by one yard wide. I myself have seen the burnt mountain and the stones from it and the burn extends for more than a quarter of a league. And when I saw this marvel I called together the chief and most ancient Indians of the village of Cacha and asked them about it; they told me what I have recounted. The *huaca* of this Viracocha is a stone's throw to the right of the burn on a level patch the other side of a stream which runs between it and the burn. Many persons have crossed the stream and have seen the *huaca* and the stone.

'I asked them what their tradition had to tell about the appearance of the Viracocha when he was seen by the first men of their race and they told me he was a man of tall stature clothed in a white robe which came down to his feet and which he wore belted at the waist. He had short hair and a tonsure like a priest. He went unshod and carried in his hands a thing which, in the light of what they know today, they liken to the breviaries which priests carry. And I asked them what was the name of the person in whose honour that stone was set up and they told me it was Con

Ticci Viracocha Pachayachachic, which means in their language "God, Creator of the World".

'To return to our story. They say that after this miracle in the district of Cacha he went on his way, intent on his work, until he came to a place which is now called the Tambo of Urcos, six leagues from Cuzco, and there he climbed a high mountain peak and sat down on the top of it. From there he commanded to be produced and to come forth from that height the Indians who today live in that region. And in that place, because Viracocha sat down there, they have made a very rich and sumptuous *huaca*. They have made there a throne of fine gold and the statue which they have set up in honour of Viracocha – also of fine gold – sits on the throne.

'From there Viracocha pursued his way, calling forth the races of men, until he came to Cuzco. There he made a Lord, to whom he gave the name Alcaviza, and he also named the site Cuzco. After leaving injunctions how after his departure the Orejones should be produced, he passed on further to continue his work. When he came to the district of Puerto Viejo he was joined by his followers whom he had sent on before as has been said, and when they had joined him he put to sea in their company and they say that he and his people went by water as easily as they had traversed the land. There are many other things I could have writ-

ten about this Viracocha according as they were told me by the Indians, but to avoid prolixity and great idolatry and bestiality I have omitted them. . .'
Juan de Betanzos: *Suma y Narración de los Incas.*

'I declare that from childhood I have heard ancient traditions and histories and fables and barbarities of heathen times and they are as follows according to the unvarying testimony of the natives about past events.

'In the age of *Purunpacha* [the savage world] all the tribes of the *Tahuantinsuyu* [the four parts of the Inca empire, i.e. the inhabited world] came from beyond Potosí in four or five armies prepared for war. As they advanced they settled in the various districts. This period was called *Ccallacpacha* or *Tutayacpacha* [the beginning of the world; or the age of darkness]. Since each band chose a place where to make its home they called this *Purunpacharacyaptin* [multitudes before the age of savagery]. This age lasted a vast number of years. As the people poured into the country there was a shortage of land and wars and quarrels became frequent. Then they began to make fortresses and there were daily clashes and the people knew no peace. Then it was that in the middle of the night they heard the *Hapi-ñuñus* [demons: lit. seizers of women's bosoms] making off with mournful cries and saying: "We are defeated! We are defeated! Ah that we should lose our subjects!" We are to understand by this that the demons had been conquered by Jesus Christ upon Calvary. For they say that in ancient times, in the age of savagery, the *Hapi-ñuñus*

74

walked to an fro in visible form over all the land so that it was not safe to go abroad at night, for they carried off men, women and children like the enemies of the human race they are.

'Some while after the devils called *Hapi-ñuñus Achacallas* had been driven from the land, there arrived in these territories of the *Tahuantinsuyu* a bearded man of medium height and long hair dressed in a rather long cloak. They say he was past his prime, with grey hair, and lean. He walked with a staff and addressed the natives with love, calling them his sons and daughters. As he traversed all the land he worked miracles. He healed the sick by his touch. He spoke every tongue even better than the natives. They called him *Thunupa* or *Tarapaca ... Viracocharapacha yachipachan* or *Pachaccan* [chief steward]. This means servant, and *Vicchaycamayoc*, which means preacher. He preached to the people but they took little notice, for they held him in low account. He was called *Thunupa Viracocha nipachan*, but surely he was the glorious apostle St Thomas.

'They say that this man came to a village called Apo-tampu [this is *Paccari-tambo*], very weary, and they were celebrating a marriage feast there. The chief listened to his teaching in a friendly spirit but the people were unwilling to listen. The traveller became a guest of the chief Apo-tampu, to whom he gave a branch from his staff, and under the influence of the chief the people heard him willingly. . .

'This good man Thunupa visited all the districts of the Collasuyu, preaching always to the people, until one day he came to the town of Yamquisupa. There he was treated with contempt and driven out. He often slept in the open without any covering but his cloak and a book. He cursed that town and it was submerged in the water. The place is now called *Yamquisupaloiga*. It is now a lake and the Indians knew that it had once been a village. On a high hill called *Cacha-pucara* [the fortress of Cacha, a town in the valley of Vilcamayo] there was an idol shaped like a woman and Thunupa disliked it bit-

terly, set fire to it and destroyed it with the hill on which it stood. The signs of this awful miracle are said to be visible today.

'Another time he began to preach with loving words in a town where they were celebrating a wedding, and they would not listen to him. Therefore he cursed them and turned them into stones, which are still to be seen. The same thing occurred at Pucara and other places. They say further that when in his wandering Thunupa came to the mountains of Caravaya he set up a large cross and carried it on his back to the mountain of Carapucu, where he preached in a loud voice and wept. The daughter of the chief had water sprinkled on her head, which was misunderstood by the Indians. So Thunupa was put in prison and his head was shorn, near the great lake of Carapucu. The name Carapucu is derived from the *pucu-pucu*, a bird which sings at dawn. When Thunupa was in prison they say that at daybreak a beautiful youth came to him and said: "Fear not, for I come to you from the mistress, who watches over you and who is about to go to the place of rest." So saying he touched with his fingers the bonds which bound Thunupa hand and foot. There were many guards, for Thunupa had been condemned to a cruel death, but at five in the morning he entered the lake with the youth, his mantle bearing him up on the waters in place of a boat.

'When he reached the town of Carapucu the leaders were annoyed that their idol had been cast down and destroyed. They say that the idol flew like the wind to a deserted place which was never visited. There the idol or *huaca* was mourning and lamenting with lowered head and was so found by an Indian, and his story made the chiefs excited at the arrival of Thunupa, who had been put in prison. They say that after he had been freed from these savage men Thunupa remained for a long time on a rock called Titicaca and then went by Tiquina to Chacamarca, where he came to a town called Tiahuanaco. The people of that town were singing and dancing when he came and were

unwilling to listen to his preaching. Then in anger he denounced them in their own language and when he left the people were turned to stone, as they can be seen to this day. This is told by the ancient Incas.' Juan de Santa Cruz Pachacuti-Yamqui Salcamayhua: *An Account of the Antiquities of Peru*.

Cosmological Myths
The cosmological stories recorded from the Collao have much in common with those from other parts of the Central Andes but with some characteristic features of their own. In many cases they have come to us conflated with legends of Inca origins and it seems that the Inca took over these legends among others to explain and justify the supremacy they arrogated to themselves. The basic form of the myth ran somewhat as follows.

In the most ancient times the earth was covered in darkness and there was no sun. For some crime unstated the people who lived in those times were destroyed by the creator. Or they were destroyed in a deluge. After the deluge the creator (or his divine embodiment) appeared in human form from Lake Titicaca. He then created the sun and moon and stars. After that he renewed the human population of the earth. He first fashioned in stone prototypes of the different races, paying great attention to details of costume and deportment.

In the Central Andean highlands the natives of each district, sometimes even each village, are distinguished by small differences of costume, chiefly headdress and hair-styles. This custom persists to some extent even today. To many, a state of affairs in which a person's place of origin is not apparent from his costume is synonymous with anarchy. The origin of the practice is sometimes attributed to the Inca. However, many myths describing human origins and dating from pre-Inca times, as this one, lay great emphasis upon it.

Tribes of living people corresponding to these prototypes were then brought forth by the creator from rocks and rivers, caves, trees and fountains through the length and

breadth of the highlands. To these he gave names and instructions in civilised life. In some versions he acts alone and in others in conjunction with subordinate divine beings who put his instructions into effect. The method of creation depicted in this and similar myths points pretty clearly to a race memory of a period of religious animism, a stage when people ascribed spiritual powers to natural features to which they attributed their origin as a group and to which they were specially attached in a symbolic way. The *huaca* in this most primitive sense was a natural

Illimani, one of the majestic peaks of the Cordillera Real which are worshipped as *Achachilas*, objects of reverence in Aymara mythology and religion. Illimani, which overlooks La Paz, is regarded as the tutelary spirit of the city and is said to be the favourite of Viracocha.

feature or object to which all the group gave particular reverence and which they connected with both the origin of the group and its continued safekeeping.

Achachilas

Among the Aymara who still inhabit the Bolivian highlands, natural objects of reverence are called *Achachilas*. Chief among them are the great mountain peaks of the Cordillera: Illimani, Illampu, Huaynu Potosí, and the rest. The Aymara Indians still perform acts of worship to them, claim them as tribal ancestors and tell traditional fables about them. People have often seen Indians, travelling by lorry from Lake Titicaca to La Paz, remove their woollen caps and take up the attitude of prayer when they came within sight of the Cordillera. Pilgrims to the shrine of the Virgin at Copacabana on the Lake still make a weekly ascent of the hill Calvario, led by the *yatiri* doctor-diviners, and from the top, along with Christian ceremonies, pay tribute to the mountain peaks which are imposingly visible from there.

The story is currently told that Illimani, the mountain which looks down on La Paz, was the favourite of Viracocha and roused therefore the envy of the neighbouring peak which was taller and larger. This peak, Mururata, grumbled to Viracocha, who in anger broke off its top with his sling so that it is now truncated, and the upper part sailed through the air to form the present Sajama. Both the Omasuyus and the Pacajes claim Illimani as their ancestor.

When two peaks stand facing each other Indian myth often represents them as male and female, as with the two mountains Sicasica and Churuquilla, *Achachilas* for the Sucre region. The natives of this region believe that the spirit of the former shows itself from time to time, and particularly at night, in the form of a young and beautiful female, who smiles seductively at those who come upon her but who cannot be approached. Indians who are found dead in these mountains are believed to have been punished for not showing due reverence towards this mountain spirit. The mountains San Juan de Parichata and Tata-Turqui outside Potosí are also worshipped as *Achachilas*, male and female, of the region. As an instance of the continuation of the native mythopoeic fancy during colonial times, the following story about Parichata may be told. It is given by M. Rigoberto Paredes in his *Mitos, Supersticiones y Supervivencias populares de Bolivia*.

Formerly the Spaniards worked silver mines on Parichata and treated the Indian labourers so harshly that in despair they appealed to the mountain. The mountain took pity on them and resolved to help them. One night an Indian muleteer was mounting the path up the mountain when he heard the clatter of carrier animals. An Indian met him and told him to go back under pain of death as the road ahead was blocked. This he did. But later he returned to the place and hiding beside the path, he saw go by an enormous troop of mules laden with silver ore. One of the beasts collapsed under its load. The muleteer went to its aid and found it had broken a bone of its shin. He therefore unloaded the silver and, taking care to mark the spot, returned to his lodging. Next day he returned but both the silver and the mule had disappeared. In the place where the mule had been lying was a beetle moving painfully with a broken leg. The spirit of the mountain had transformed all the beetles of the region into mules to cart away all the silver ore in the mountain. From that night the veins of silver in Parichata

Right. Detail of woven textile from Paracas Necropolis in the southern coastal zone of Peru, about 400–100 B.C. It appears to represent three demon figures half humorously conceived. The long trailers descending from the headdresses terminate in conventional snake heads. The figures carry what may be a ceremonial axe or knife in one hand and a bent staff, whose significance is lost, in the other.

Opposite. Neither the provenance nor the interpretation of this curious terracotta is known. It appears to represent a boat; not the usual balsa boat made from the totora rush, but a boat of skins. In it are laid out figures of the dead. It may indicate a myth comparable to Egyptian and Greek myths in which the dead were taken by boat to the other world – but in the absence of confirmatory evidence the symbolism must remain obscure. Kemper Collection.

dried up and the Indians were no longer worked to death mining it for the Spaniards. The silver was removed to Tata-Turqui, where it was mined until recently, but the abuse of the Indians ceased.

Some tribes still trace their first beginnings from lakes. Thus the Quillacas say they are descendants of Lake Poopo, sacred to the moon. The despised Urus, whose language is not Aymara, are said to have been born from the slime of Lake Titicaca when it was first heated by the sun. Yet another tradition holds that the Urus were originally transplanted from the Pacific coast as slaves and settled near Titicaca by a chieftain called Tacuilla.

Good and Evil Spirits

The modern Indians of the Andean highlands retain a deeply embedded belief in good and evil spirits, which are called Machulas or also Achachilas when they are attached to some natural feature. These are sometimes identified with spirits of famous men remembered from the past. In both cases these spirits may be either localised or freely wandering without any specific local habitation. When drinking spirits or chewing coca the Indian will pour a few drops as a libation or scatter a few coca leaves to avert the anger of the spirits. Travellers pour a libation to the spirits of

Above. The monument known as the Huaca del Sol (Temple of the Sun), outside the modern town of Trujillo, the largest and most impressive of the enormous ceremonial structures in the form of platforms surmounted by terraced pyramids built of adobe bricks by the Moche people. The base platform measures 750 feet by 450 feet and is 60 feet high (228 m x 137 m x 18 m). It rises up in five terraces and is surmounted by a stepped pyramidal structure 340 feet square (104 m) and 75 feet (23 m) high. It has been estimated to contain 130 million adobe bricks. The Mochica culture of the northern coast of Peru was roughly contemporary with Paracas and Nazca in the southern coastal area about 300 B.C. to A.D. 500. It was preceded by the Gallinazo and, after a period of Tiahuanaco influence, was succeeded by Chimu. It was centred in the same area as the Chimu empire, the valleys of Chicama, Moche, Viru and Santa.

Opposite left. Mochica stirrup vase representing a human figure playing a drum. The mutilated nostrils and lips and the cuts on either side of the mouth would seem to indicate some ceremonial punishment, perhaps of a captured enemy. Kemper Collection.

Opposite right. Mochica whistling jar of red ceramic representing a house or shelter within which are a man and a suckling mother. Birds are perched on the corners of the roof, and the roof tiles are decorated with relief modelling. Kemper Collection.

mountain passes, peaks, defiles, pools, curiously shaped crags, etc. In some cases, particularly at local cemeteries, called Chullperios, more or less continuous rites are celebrated with symbolic gifts of food and drink offered to avert the anger of the spirits should they go hungry.

The malignant spirits, called Anchancho, are dreaded. Their counterparts, the Ekkekko, are the source of good luck and success. Oblitas Poblete records a legend that both the Anchancho and the Ekkekko were children of a powerful prince, the Mallcu of Chacamita, the Ekkekko by his legitimate wife, Curaj Mama, and the Anchancho by concubines.

The spirits of evil are believed to be responsible for all illnesses and diseases and are sometimes spoken of almost as if they were considered to be spirits of disease. They can enter and take possession of people when the soul (Jukkui Ajayo) leaves the body in sleep or owing to sudden fright and they can then cause illness, exhaustion and death. They also have the power of the evil eye, by which they can charm a person and then enter their body and suck the heart's blood, causing death. Twilight (which

is short in the Andes) is a particularly dangerous time, when special care must be taken to avoid the Anchancho. These spirits also frequent solitary mountain places, particularly during storms, and there their voice may sometimes be heard like the braying of an ass.

The dangerous and evil spirits are sometimes collectively identified with the Supay, which the early chroniclers identified with the Christian devil. He is sometimes described as a monster with a lion's body, ram's horns, tiger's teeth, and hooves and emits a smell of sulphur. (The elements of accretion are here apparent). He can change himself into a cat or a pig or an owl and he can inhabit natural phenomena like the earthquake or hurricane or storm. When he is angry he may roar like a wild cat and at other times he grunts like a pig. But he can also take the form of a handsome youth or maiden and then, after gaining a person's confidence, will enter his body and cause epilepsy or madness. The main concern of the Supay is to damage human beings. He is also the Lord of mineral wealth and can change veins of silver into quartz or gold to pyrites.

The counterpart of the Supay is the Ekkekko, a domestic god of good luck and prosperity, who is represented by small figures of a bald, pot-bellied man radiating happiness and goodwill, usually loaded with all manner of objects of domestic and personal use. Going back to before the Conquest, when figures of the Ekkekko were made in silver and gold, the cult of the Ekkekko has always been connected with things in miniature. Small figures of the Ekkekko had a place of honour in every Indian household during the Colonial period and are still popular today. He often wears a little red poncho and a peaked cap. In his *Vocabulario de la Lengua Aymará* Ludovico Bertonio connects him with the god Thunupa, and says that the Indians tell innumerable stories about the good fortune caused by the Ekkekko. Tiny figures of the god are widely worn as amulets and charms.

The cult of the Ekkekko is especially connected with the annual fairs in La Paz, Cochabamba and Oruro called Alacitas. At these fairs all things are sold in miniature and are much sought after by the natives and cholos. An Indian or a chola woman,

for example, will buy a miniature pottery house at the Alacitas in order to make certain that she will obtain a husband and a house of her own. The La Paz festival of Alacitas is said to derive from a fair instituted by Sebastian de Segurola in 1781 to celebrate the relief of the city from siege by Tupac Catari during the insurrection of Tupac Amaru. The belief in the Ekkekko and the associated mythology are much older than this, however, and very widely disseminated in the Andean region.

According to one myth the capital of the kingdom of the Ekkekko is a miniature city whose ruins may be seen on the heights of Suttilaya, in the Province of Bautista Saavedra, Department of La Paz.

High Gods
The Indians of South America had no clearly personified gods around whom cycles of myth accumulated, like the Greek gods of Olympus. Oblitas Poblete speaks of a supreme deity, Tutujanawin 'the Beginning and the End of All Things,' and describes him as the principle of energy which sustains the universe and gives life and movement to all things. Associ-

ated with him was the god Inti or Pachatata, who was the creator of mankind and who governs the stars in the firmament. Associated with him again, as his wife or sister, was Pachamama, the goddess of fecundity who gives life to animals and men, sustaining nature in all its manifestations. There is also in many parts a belief in Chuquiilla, god of the storm, who together with Yllappa and Lliphi-Lliphi, personifications of the thunderbolt, controls the weather and causes storm, hurricane and lightning when he is enraged. This group of gods are appeased by offerings of alcohol, coca and the fat of llamas.

The Human Soul
The beliefs of the highland Indians incorporate no precisely organised doctrines about the human soul or life after death and attempts to summarise or systematise these beliefs inevitably fail to do justice to their fluid and imprecise character. If there ever existed a more highly organised body of belief, this has been lost beyond recall in the mists of time. The modern Indian retains a vaguely apprehended tradition upon which has been superimposed an only half

understood corpus of Christian doctrine. The beliefs that may have existed before the Spanish conquest interested the early chroniclers only to the extent that they seemed to confirm or contradict Christian teaching.

It is clear that the South American Indians have inherited a belief in two different souls which inhabit the human body, though there is no clearly worked out doctrine. There is on the one hand the Life Spirit, Athun Ajayo, which is derived from Pachamama or Pacasmili, and bestows the power of movement, consciousness and all that is implied by life. If this soul departs, the body dies. It is presumably this soul which survives the death of the body. The Jukkui Ajayo or Pipisao, on the other hand, is responsible for keeping body and mind in a state of health. It is able to leave the body during sleep and wander around the world, transmitting its impressions in the form of dreams. If it fails to return to the body at the right time, or if it is forced from the body by sudden shock or fright, the body is left susceptible to attacks by the evil spirits of disease.

When a person dies their soul (Athun Ajayo) remains in the house for the eight days of mourning, eating with the family. It returns after a year (or among Christian Indians on the Feast of All Saints), when it must take in enough sustenance to last over until the next return. Special meals are supplied for the returned Ajayos. There is a belief that the souls dislike going to the other world alone and

are apt to take with them unmarried persons; therefore it is thought advisable for bachelors and spinsters to avoid the house during the eight days of mourning and on the days when the Ajayos return. Not entirely consistent with these beliefs, there exists a ritualistic practice of offering symbolic food and drink to the souls at the cemeteries and there exists also a belief that some at least of the souls of the departed continue to exist as localised spirits attached to specific places or striking natural features.

The practice of mummifying the bodies of Inca kings and the extensive burials that have been discovered in the coastal districts of Peru and elsewhere seem to indicate that some belief in a future life was prevalent before the Spanish Conquest. But in the centuries that have elapsed since the Conquest beliefs in an after life have been so overlaid and transformed by Christian teaching that it is no longer possible to recover the pre-Christian beliefs and mythology. We can be sure only of a persisting belief that the souls of the departed require ritualistic attention, that this was sometimes associated with a cult of ancestors and famous men of the past and that at any rate some spirits of the dead became localised deities of rocks, streams, lakes, mountains and other natural features.

Thunupa

The mythological cycle of the Collao also contains stories of a culture hero, the bringer of civilisation and an advanced social code. He is variously named Thunupa, Tonapa and Taapac. Although a fair amount is told about him, it is excessively difficult to disentangle for several reasons. First, many of his activities are elsewhere attributed to Viracocha, the creator-god, and no clear distinction of function is made between them. Second, the official Inca syncretistic mythology arrogated to the founders of the Inca dynasty the attributes of a culture hero and sought to heighten the prestige of the dynasty by connecting its origin with Titicaca and the Collao. Thus the Thunupa myth was conflated with the myth of Inca origins. Thirdly, much of our information about the myth comes from the researches of the Augustinian Fathers (themselves by no means lacking in credulity), and in particular Antonio de la Calancha's *Crónica moralizada del orden de San Agustín en el Perú*, which was published in 1638.

Indian legend was still plastic and creative during the Colonial period and there is no doubt that many of the attributes ascribed to Thunupa in the stories preserved by Calancha were assimilated to the stories told by the Fathers to the Indians about the Apostles. Even Salcamayhua and Guamán Poma de Ayala were Christian converts. The former identifies Thunupa with St Thomas and the latter with St Bartholomew. So the *persona* of Thunupa acquires a twofold character in the stories. On the one hand he is the acme of loving kindness and invites martyrdom. On the other hand when he is angered or rejected he punishes the guilty ones by turning them to stone or drowning them in a flood. The myth runs as follows.

Thunupa appeared on the Altiplano in ancient times, coming from the north with five disciples. He was a man of august presence, blue-eyed, bearded, without headgear and wearing a *cusma*, a jerkin or sleeveless shirt reaching to the knees. He was sober, puritanical and preached against drunkenness, polygamy and war. He first came carrying a large wooden cross on his back to Carapucu, the capital of the famous chief Makuri, and reproved the latter for his warlike deeds and his cruelty. Makuri took no account of him, but the priests and soothsayers set up an opposition to him. Thunupa then went to Sicasica, where his preaching annoyed the people and they set fire

to the house where he was sleeping. Escaping from the fire, Thunupa returned to Carapucu. But during his absence one of his disciples had fallen in love with and converted the daughter of Makuri, and on his return Thunupa had her baptised. Angered at this, Makuri martyred the disciples and left Thunupa for dead. Calancha then takes up the story:

'They put his blessed body in a boat of totora rush and set it adrift on Lake Titicaca. [Totora is a strong rush which grows on the shores of Lake Titicaca. The Indians fashion it into bundles from which they still make their boats.] There the gentle waters served him for oars and the soft winds for pilot, and he sailed away with such speed that those who had tried so cruelly to kill him were left behind in terror and astonishment. For this lake has no current. . . The boat came to the shore at Cochamarca, where today is the river Desaguadero. Indian tradition asserts that the boat struck the land with such force it created the river Desaguadero, which before then did not exist. And on the water so released the holy body was carried many leagues away to the sea coast at Arica.'

There was also a tradition that his enemies tried to destroy Thunupa's cross, both by fire and by hewing it to pieces, but were unable to do so. They tried to get rid of it in the Lake but it would not sink. They then buried it in the ground and it was unearthed and discovered to the Augustine Fathers in 1569, as related by Ramos Gavilán in *Historia del célebre y milagroso Santuario de la insigne imagen de Nuestra Señora de Copacabana*, published in 1621.

In his *Account of the Antiquities of Peru* Salcamayhua tells of a visit by the Inca monarch Capac Yupanqui to the highlands around Titicaca.

'It is said that the Inca sent men to search for the place called Titicaca, where the great Thunupa had arrived, and that they brought water thence to pour over the infant Inca Roca while they celebrated the praises of Thunupa. [This is the only account I have found pointing to a cult of

Thunupa.] In the spring on the top of the rocks the water was in a basin called *ccapacchama quispisutuc una* [rich joy of crystal drops of water]. Future Incas caused this water to be brought in a bowl called *curi-ccacca* (rock of gold) and placed in the middle of the square of Cuzco called Huacay-pata, where they did honour to the water which had been touched by Thunupa.

'In those days the *curacas* [village headmen] of Asillu and Hucuru told the Inca how in ancient times a poor thin old man with a beard and long hair had come to them in a long tunic and that he was a wise counsellor in matters of state and that his name was Thunupa Vihinquira. They said that he had banished all the idols and *Hapi-ñuñu* demons to the snowy mountains. All the *curacas* and chroniclers also said that this Thunupa had banished all the idols and *huacas* to the mountains of Asancata, Quiyancatay, Sallcatay and Apitosiray. When all the *curacas* of the Tahuantinsuyu were assembled in the Huacay-pata, each in his place, those of the Huancas said that this Thunupa Varivillca had also been in their land and that he had made a house to live in and had banished all the *huacas* and *Hapi-ñuñus* in the provinces of Hatun Sausa to the snowy mountains in Pariacaca and Vallollo. Before their banishment these idols had done much harm to the people, forcing the *curacas* to make human sacrifices to them.

'The Inca ordered that the house of Thunupa should be preserved. It was at the foot of a small hill near the river as you enter Jauja from the Cuzco road, and before coming to it there are two stones where Thunupa had turned a female *huaca* into stone for having fornicated with a man of the Huancas.'

Magic Cities
Certain ethnologists have reported myths of enchanted cities and palaces endowed with a fatal allurement, myths which are not reported from pre-Conquest times and which nevertheless seem difficult to ascribe to Christian influences.

Oblitas Poblete was told by an Indian that on a lovely cone-shaped mountain peak there exists a palace of the Ñustas, daughters of the Inca and of ancient village chieftains. On a clear night amidst scenes of indescribable beauty the traveller can see these princesses dancing to the sound of celestial music. The enchantment is well-nigh irresistible, but those who succumb and approach too near are enchanted for ever and turned to stone. Similar stories are told of other abodes of divinities from the past whose superhuman charm leads unwary travellers to their doom. Among others he mentions stories of a crystal city in the mountain range of Akhamani, enchanted cities in the region of Caballuni, the mountain peak of Tuana and in the heights of Gura-Gura. At night the sounds of dancing and revelry can be heard from these cities but it is impossible to approach them under pain of death. Many 'enchantments' are linked with stories of divinely beautiful girls or youths, wonderful fruits or gardens of flowers, which lure incautious travellers to their destruction.

Vicuña Cifuentes tells a rather similar story of the enchanted 'City of the Caesars' in the mountains of southern Chile. It is said to be a magnificent city of gold and silver and precious stones, where no-one is born and no-one dies. The inhabitants live a life of ease and luxury without the need to work. Those who reach this city lose all memory of their past and remain there for ever – or if people do leave it, they lose memory of what they saw there. The myth is sometimes traced to the story of Captain Francisco César, who in 1528 went with fourteen companions to explore the mountains of southern Chile for mines. But if so, the mythical elements are surprisingly similar to the 'enchanted cities' recorded by Oblitas Poblete and the story may have been conflated with an existing myth.

Among other 'Enchantments' Vicuña Cifuentes mentions the following: In the lagoon of Pudahuel a wagoner was enchanted together with the ox-cart and the oxen he was driving. This happened because he tried

to cross the lake; as he advanced the lake receded and when he came to the middle the waters engulfed him. Afterwards this famous lake began to dry up and became muddy and the Enchantment, together with all the fishes in it, was translated in a cloud to the lake Aculeo, where it now is. In this lake Aculeo it is said that there is an enchanted princess, who has been seen combing the golden tresses of her lovely hair with a golden comb.

A farm hand came upon a palace in the mountains and was invited to enter by invisible voices. He remained there several days, delighting in the contemplation of its riches, strolling freely through the parks and avenues and taking his pleasure in the entertainments provided by his unknown hosts. When he wanted to leave his invisible friends told him that he could return whenever he liked on the sole condition that he told no-one what he had seen, and in memory of his sojourn among them they gave him a beautiful gold horn to serve as a drinking cup. But the richness of this present excited the curiosity of those who saw it and they did not desist until they had extracted the secret from the good man. From that moment many went to the mountains in search of the palace and the man himself tried several times to return. But none of them could find any trace of the marvellous edifice. The palace was enchanted and had changed its locality when its secret was divulged.

From *Chiloé y los Chilotes* (1914) by Francisco J. Cavada comes the story that at the time of the discovery of the placer mines at Hornohuinco there was rumour of an enchanted mountain all of solid gold, but it was defended by an invisible power, a mysterious agent who did not allow access to it.

Whether of native or of Spanish origin, these stories of enchantment, which have gained currency among the Indian population, reveal a strange family likeness.

Coca

The coca plant has been cultivated from time immemorial in the semitropical valleys of the Andean Cor-

Mochica stirrup vase with skull head wearing the usual 'snood' headdress tied beneath the chin. Painted on the body are a coca pouch like the *chuspa* in which the modern Indian carries his daily coca ration, and hands holding a chilli pepper, or *aci*. The custom of representing a death's head, often in conjunction with living figures, has persisted to the present day, though its significance is no longer understood. Kemper Collection.

On pages 86–7. Feathered cloak with Jaguar design. Nazca period. Elaborate feathered cloaks from the tropical interior were among the finery boasted by dignitaries of the coastal kingdoms and the Inca. Museum of Mankind, London.

dilleras. The dried leaves of the coca are masticated by the Indians and produce a state of euphoria which, they believe, enables them to sustain hunger, cold and fatigue. Coca leaves have been found in early coastal burials. During Inca times it was known as the 'divine plant' and it is said that its use was reserved for the Inca aristocracy. But the habit of chewing

coca was so general and so ingrained among the native population even in the first decades of the Conquest that attempts to eradicate it were ineffective and to this day its cultivation is a major part of agricultural industry in Bolivia. (For a fuller account, see the author's *Indians of the Andes*, pp. 237-51.)

Cieza de León wrote about it as follows. 'In Peru, in all its extent, it was the custom, and is, to carry this coca in the mouth and from morning until they retire to sleep they carry it without emptying it from their mouths. And when I enquired of certain Indians why they keep their mouths ever filled with that herb (the which they eat not neither do they more than carry it between their teeth), they say that they have little sense of hunger and feel great vigour and strength. For my part I believe that it must have some effect, though rather indeed it seems a vicious custom and the sort to be expected of a people such as these Indians are. In the Andes from Huamanga to the town of Plata this coca is cultivated and it grows on small bushes which they tend much and cherish that they shall produce the leaf they call coca; and they dry it in the sun and then pack it in certain long and narrow bales, each one a little over one arroba [about 25 lbs]... There are some in Spain now rich with the profits they have made from this coca, buying it up and selling it to the markets of the Indians.'

Coca is the object of semi-religious awe and reverence among the Indians. The leaves were used by the wise men or *amautas* for divination and were burnt as a sacred fumigant before religious ceremonies and to purify suspected places from evil spirits or the spirits of diseases. They were offered in ritual sacrifices to the gods, to propitiate the earth goddess Pachamama, and to ward off ill luck. A tincture of coca is thought to have been one of the ingredients in the process of mummification practised by the Inca and still imperfectly understood. Plasters of coca leaves were applied, then as now, to wounds and contusions, and infusions of coca

were given as a remedy for stomach and intestinal afflictions.

Among the modern Indians coca has lost nothing of its former medical and magical importance. It is still used by the diviner (*yatiri*) to foretell the future and by the magician (*pako*) and the doctor (*kollasiri*) to diagnose the cause of disease. Coca is still offered to Pachamama to ensure her favour for the crops and to bring good luck when a new house is built. Coca leaves are offered to the dead and to all the supernatural powers. A simple offering consists of six perfect leaves placed green side up one above the other (*aita*). A more elaborate offering consists of 144 *aita* in twelve rows of twelve. The most perfect offering of all is to burn a block of llama fat with coca at midnight inside a ring of dried llama dung and to throw the ashes into a stream. Today as heretofore coca is no less an essential part of the ritual life of the Indian than it is a daily necessity and indulgence.

For the purpose of divination the Yatiri first breathes deeply on to a bundle of good quality coca in order to transmit his magic power to it. He then places the coca in the breast of the enquirer for five minutes or so in order to create a rapport between them. When this is done he selects twelve perfect coca leaves and arranges them in a row on a cloak (*aguayo*), marking each to represent

---

a person, animal, place, etc. Twelve other leaves are then dropped on to them. If the leaves fall with the front side upwards, the luck is good; if they fall with the reverse upwards, misfortune is portended. If the leaves fall in a row, one result is foretold; if they make a cross the significance is different. And so on, sometimes with quite elaborate complications.

There are two myths told of the origin of coca. One, referred to by the Peruvianist Julio Tello, comes from a report of the Viceroy Toledo (1568-72). 'About its origin they all say they know nothing except six who say that among the natives there was a legend that before the coca tree was as it is now there was a beautiful woman and because she lived a loose life they slew her and cut her in two. From her body grew the bush which they call Mama-coca and from that time they began to eat it. They carried it in a small bag and it was forbidden to open the bag and eat it until after they had had relations with a woman in memory of that woman. For this reason they call it coca.'

Another legend says that Indians of the Altiplano found their way over the crest of the mountains and settled

in the high valleys, called Yungas, of the eastern slopes of the Cordillera. In order to clear land for cultivation, they set fire to the teeming forest and undergrowth. The smoke from the fires rose and polluted the peaks of Illimani and Illampu, the ice-mansions of Khuno, the god of snow and storm. Angered at this, Khuno sent down torrential rain and hail on the Yungas, which destroyed the houses and farms, opened up ravines and caused swift rivers and streams which swept everything away. They also destroyed the mountain roads and cut off the Indians from the highlands. Coming out from the caves in which they had taken refuge, the Indians found nothing but desolation around them until, weak with hunger and despair, they at last came upon an unknown shrub with leaves of a brilliant green. Gathering the leaves of this plant, they put them in their mouths to stay their hunger and immediately were invaded by a sense of supreme wellbeing. They no longer felt the hunger, the weariness or the cold. Refreshed with new energy, they were able to return to Tiahuanaco, where they revealed the secret of this wonderful new plant to the elders (*auquis*) and wise men (*amautas*); and thus the knowledge of coca spread throughout the sierra. (José Agustin Morales, *El Oro Verde de los Yungas*, 1938, and M. Rigoberto Paredes, *Mitos, Supersticiones y Supervivencias populares de Bolivia*, 1963.)

Myths and Legends of the Coast

High Gods

As we have seen, before the introduction of Christianity the highland peoples of Peru worshipped a High God called Viracocha, whom they represented as the supreme creator of all things and sometimes also as a culture hero who instructed the newly created peoples of the earth in the arts of civilisation. A similar High God called Con or Coniraya was recognised among the coastal peoples, although less information has been preserved about his functions and attributes. The myths reported by Francisco de Avila and Francisco López de Gomara are not very revealing.

Another High God was worshipped under the name of Pachacamac at a temple built on a small hill in a fertile coastal valley of the same name four leagues south of the site of the modern city of Lima. The cult was earlier than the Inca religion of the Sun in the coastal valleys of Peru and had great prestige, rivalling that of Tiahuanaco. A powerful priesthood was attached to the temple and the ritual included sacrifices and an oracle. Pachacamac was worshipped only at this one temple, which was a centre of pilgrimage from many parts of the country. Pilgrims brought gifts to the god and it was held to be an honour to be buried in the vicinity of the temple. So great was the prestige of this cult and the reputed wealth of the temple that when the Inca conquests reached the valley of Pachacamac they did not suppress the cult and replace it by the cult of the Sun, as was their usual habit in conquered territories, but joined the cult of Pachacamac with their own worship of the Sun. The temple was later sacked by Hernando Pizarro but, as the story goes, the Indian priests were able to remove and bury the temple treasures before they fell into the hands of the Conquistadors.

The Inca Garcilaso de la Vega says in the *Comentarios reales de los Incas* (Book 1, chap. 11): 'If I were asked today what is the name of God in your language, I would reply "Pachacamac," for in the general language of Peru there is no other word which so well expresses the concept of God.' Cieza de León derives the name from *camac*, creator, and *pacha*, the world. Garcilaso disagrees with this and says that *camac* means 'animator' or 'giver of life.' Describing the great respect in which Pachacamac was held, Garcilaso says: 'They held his name in great reverence, not daring to utter it aloud. Or if they had to do so, they made gestures of honour and veneration, hunching the shoulders, bowing the head and the whole body, raising their eyes to the Heavens and lowering them to the earth, lifting the open hands to the level of the shoulders and casting kisses into the air. These were signs of great reverence among them, which they also used towards the Sun and the Inca nobility. . .'

Cieza de León gives the following account.

'Four leagues from the City of the Kings [Lima], travelling down the coast, is the valley of Pachacamac, which is very famous among these Indians. This valley is fruitful and pleasant and in it there was one of the grandest temples that is to be seen in this part of the world. They say that although the Incas built many other

Terracotta female figurine from the coastal valley of Chancay in an attitude which may express adoration or prayer.

Above. A street in Cuzco surviving from Inca times. The remarkable use of cut stone blocks is plainly seen and, on the lintel, two serpents. According to Guamán Poma de Ayala the people of this period believed that snakes (and foxes) had the power to absorb evil, drawing it away from man. The snakes seen here were probably a device to protect the family who lived there.

Left. A tintinabulum fashioned out of copper and surmounted by the head of possibly a chief or priest. North coast of Peru. Musée de l'Homme, Paris.

Opposite. Mochica stirrup vase with relief modelling representing what may be either a warrior slaying an opponent or a scene of ritualistic sacrifice. The standing figure has a tail or pendant terminating in a snake's head and the face with prominent fangs may indicate a jaguar mask. On the other hand the 'defeated' figure also carries what seems to be an axe and this would indicate a scene of combat. Kemper Collection.

temples besides that of Cuzco and embellished them with great riches, none equalled that of Pachacamac. It was built on a small artificial hill made of adobe and soil. The temple had many doors and both they and the walls were painted with figures of fierce animals. Inside, where they placed the idol, were the priests, who pretended to much sanctity. When they performed the sacrifices before the multitude of people they went with their faces towards the doors and their backs to the idol, with eyes cast down and filled with great awe and trembling. . . They say that they sacrificed many animals and some human beings before the statue of this demon, and that in their most solemn rituals it gave oracular replies which were accepted as truth. The priests were held in great reverence and the chiefs and caciques obeyed them in many things.

'The report goes that near the temple there used to be many rooms built for the pilgrims and that only the chiefs and pilgrims bringing gifts were considered worthy to be buried in the temple vicinity. At the annual festivals a great concourse of people assembled and amused themselves to the sound of music.

'It was the custom of the Inca to build temples to the Sun in all the territories they conquered. But when they came to Pachacamac, seeing the majesty and antiquity of this temple and the respect and devotion it aroused in all the neighbourhood, they thought it would be very difficult to abolish it and therefore agreed to its continuance on condition that a temple to the Sun was set aside on the loftiest part... When the governor Don Francisco Pizarro (God permitting it) seized Atahuallpa in the province of Cajamarca, hearing wonderful reports of this temple and the quantity of riches that were there, he sent his brother Captain Hernando Pizarro with a force of Spaniards to seek it out and seize the gold that was there. And although Hernando made all diligence, it is common talk among the Indians that the chiefs and priests of the temple had already taken off more than four hundred loads of gold before he arrived. This has not reappeared and the Indians alive today don't know where it is... From the time that Hernando Pizarro and other Christians entered this temple the devil has had little power and the idols that were there have been destroyed. The buildings, including the temple to the Sun, have fallen into ruins and few people now remain in the district.'

No more than such tantalising hints of the Pachacamac and Coniraya mythological cycles have survived. We know nothing in detail about the attributes of these gods or the nature of the associated beliefs. Our information is just as sparse about the mythology which prevailed in the coastal culture of Chavín and the great kingdoms of Mochica and Chimu which preceded the Inca. The many burials which have been discovered in the coastal valleys, well stocked with funerary ceramics and other equipment, strongly suggest belief in an after life and perhaps a cult of the dead. But we know nothing in detail about it or the associated mythology. The prevalence of a stylised Jaguar figure in representations of all kinds may well be an indication of a Jaguar god and a Jaguar cult. But again we can only speculate about the associated beliefs and mythology. In these circumstances it is impossible to reconstruct a coherent system of mythology and we must perforce be content with mentioning some of the

isolated myths which happen to have survived.

The Invasion of Giants
Cieza de León records the following story of an invasion of giants, which he heard from the natives of Santa Elena in what is now Ecuador. The Dominican friar Reginaldo de Lizárraga, who lived in Peru from 1555 to 1599 and wrote *La descripción y población de las indias*, recounts the same myth from Santa Elena more

briefly but identical in all essentials with the story of Cieza.

'As there exist rumours of giants in Peru, who landed at the point of Santa Helena, near Puerto Viejo, I will report what I have myself been told without paying attention to the stories current among the vulgar, who always exaggerate what happened. The natives recount the following tradition, which they heard from their fathers and the latter from ancient tradition.

Opposite. Woven textile from Chancay in the central coastal region of Peru. The pattern is formed from stylised feline (puma?) and bird motifs, with possibly also deer. The traditional pattern has here a purely decorative function and is treated light-heartedly and even humorously. The religious and ritualistic impact made by the feline motif in earlier Chavín and Paracas art is no longer present.

Below. Detail of the bridge of a double-spouted Chimu vase. On either side of the crowned head are frog and monkey figures. There is no portraiture in the Chimu period, and animals and birds are sometimes so formalised as to be difficult to identify. Technical skill has outlasted the spontaneity of the earlier craftsmanship. Particularly characteristic of the Chimu is a beautifully modelled black ware richly various in design and subject. Kemper Collection.

'There arrived by sea in balsa boats made of rushes [totora, see p. 46], but as large as ships, men so enormous that from the knee downwards they were the size of an ordinary man of good stature. Their limbs were in proportion to the size of their bodies and it was a monstrous thing to see their huge heads and the hair which came down to their shoulders. Their eyes were as large as saucers. They say they had no beards. Some were dressed in the skins of animals, others had no other costume than nature gave them. They brought no women with them. When they landed they made some sort of settlement at this point and the sites of their houses are still pointed out. As they found no water, they bored some extremely deep wells in the rock – a work truly worthy of remembrance, since only men of their outstanding strength could have done it. For they dug these wells in the living rock until they found water and then lined them from bottom to top with masonry such as would resist the wear and tear of time for many centuries. In these wells there is excellent and wholesome water, so cool that it is always a delight to drink.

'But these giants ate so much that they soon exhausted the resources of the district – since one of them devoured more meat than fifty of the natives. As they could not find enough to satisfy them, they slaugh-

tered large quantities of fish in the sea with their nets and other gear. They were hated by the natives because they killed their women in associating with them, and the men aslo for other causes. They leagued together to resist this new race of giants who had come to occupy their lands, but were not strong enough to engage them. So many years passed and the giants were still in the land.

'Since they lacked women and the natives would have nothing to do with them because of their size, they practised sodomy with each other openly and without shame or fear of God. . . The natives assert that God visited on them a punishment befitting the enormity of their crime. When they were all together and indulging in their homosexual practices fearful and terrifying fire came down from the sky with a huge noise and from the midst came forth a shining angel, a sharp and glittering sword in his hand. With a single blow he slew them all and the fire consumed them, so that there remained only a few bones and skulls which God permitted to stay unconsumed by the fire as a memory of this punishment.

'This they say about the giants. The which we believe is true, for in this part there have been found and are still found enormous bones, and I have heard tell of Spaniards who have

seen a piece of a tooth which complete would have weighed half a butcher's pound.' Pedro de Cieza de León: *Crónica del Perú.* I, Ch. 52.

It is curious how often allusions to a race of giants in the distant past or in distant parts of the country crop up in the writings of the early chroniclers of South America. For example the Jesuit missionary Pedro Lozano makes reference to 'giants with face like a dog and long sharp teeth' said to have been found by a certain Juan Alvarez de Maldonado in the Andes near Cuzco. The belief in giants seems to have infected even some of the explorers. For example, Antonio Pigafetta, historian of Magellan's voyage round the world (1534), describes gigantic people whom he claims to have seen himself in Patagonia: 'One day when we least expected it a man of gigantic stature presented himself to us... This man was so tall that our heads hardly reached up to his girdle... I encountered many others there... The women were less tall than the men but more fat.'

Myths of Huarochiri

Huarochiri or Warachiri is a highland district on the western side of the coastal Cordillera of Peru, east of Lima, and their own legends, as reported, indicate that the Indians migrated there in distant times from the coastal valleys. An unfinished manuscript written in Quechua in 1608 was left by Francisco de Avila, priest of San Damian, the principal parish of the district of Huarochiri. It is described by him as '*A Narrative of the Errors, False Gods, and other Superstitions and Diabolical Rites in which the Indians of the Provinces of Huarochiri, Mama and Chaclla lived in ancient times, and in which they even now live, to the great perdition of their souls*'. The fragment is a somewhat confused account of the myths and legends which survived among these people at the beginning of the seventeenth century, and was obtained by Father Avila 'from trustworthy persons who, with special diligence, ascertained the whole truth'. The manuscript was first published in the English translation by Clements R. Markham issued by the Hakluyt Society in 1873. The manu-

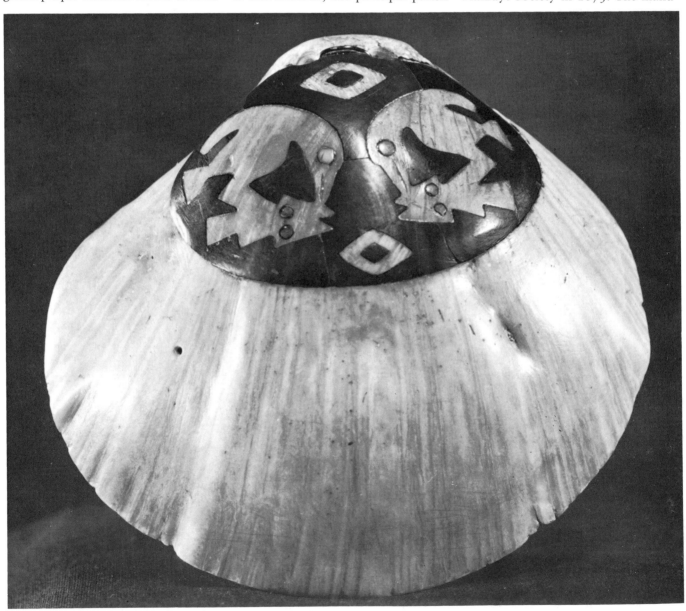

script begins as follows in Markham's translation.

'It is a most ancient tradition that, before any other event of which there is any memory, there were certain *huacas* or idols, which, together with others of which I shall treat, must be supposed to have walked in the form of men. These *huacas* were called *Yananamca Intanamca*; and in a certain encounter they had with another *huaca* called Huallallo Caruincho, they were conquered and destroyed by the said Huallallo, who remained as Lord and God of the land. He ordered that no woman should bring forth more than two children, of which one was to be sacrificed for him to eat, and the other – whichever of the two the parents chose – might be brought up. It was also a tradition that in those days all who died were brought to life again on the fifth day and that what was sown in that land also sprouted, grew, and ripened on the fifth day; and that all these three provinces were then a very hot country, which the Indians call *Yunca* or *Ande*; and they say that these crops were made visible in the deserts and uninhabited places, such as that of Pariacaca and others; and that in these Andes there was a great variety of most beautiful and brilliant birds, such as macaws, parrots and others. All this, with the people who then inhabited the land (and who, according to their account, led very evil lives), and the said idol, came to be driven away to other Andes by the idol Pariacaca, of whom I shall speak presently and of the battle he had with this Huallallo Caruincho.'

Yunca – or as it is nowadays spelled 'Yungas' – are the wet and fertile valleys of the coastal region or

---

Opposite. The peoples of South America, like those of every land and culture, used the forms of the creatures most familiar to them for their decorative art. This shell pendant is Chimu, from the north coastal plains of Peru. The inlay, showing two birds eating a fish, is turquoise. Dumbarton Oaks, Washington D.C. Robert Woods Bliss Collection.

Below. Rock engraving of a double llama, with the two heads facing in opposite directions. The masked head above may be intended to represent a Supreme Deity or a god of agriculture and cattle. Atacama desert.

the western slopes of the Cordillera. Avila rightly discredits the legend that the harsh highlands had formerly been tropical and fertile. He does not see the implication of the tradition he reports, namely that the Indians of Huarochiri had in ancient times lived on the coast and had been driven back by invaders into the highlands.

The time of primitive darkness
'A long time ago the sun disappeared and the world was dark for a space of five days. The stones knocked one against another. The mortars, which they called *mutca*, and the pestles, called *marop*, rose against their masters, who were also attacked by their sheep [llamas], both those fastened in the houses and those in the fields [i.e. wild auchenids, vicuña].'

Avila takes this to be an account of an eclipse. It may well have been, however, a myth of a time of primeval darkness analogous to the stories of the darkness before the deluge in Collao mythology.

The deluge
'An Indian tethering his llama where there was good pasture noticed that it displayed signs of grief, refusing to eat and crying *yu' yu'*. The llama told him it was sad because in five days the sea would cover the whole earth, destroying everything in it. [This prognostication of the deluge by a llama is paralleled in the account reported by Morúa.] Under the guidance of the llama the Indian went to the top of a high mountain called Villcacoto, taking food for five days. There he found so many animals and birds assembled that there was barely room for them all. The sea began to rise, the waters filled the valleys and covered all the hills except Villcacoto. They were so crowded that the fox's tail dipped into the water, which is the reason why the tips of foxes' tails are black. After five days the waters abated and from this sole survivor are descended all the people now in the world.'

Stories of Pariacaca
'At the time of the primitive anarchy called *Purunpacha* which followed

the deluge, when there was no centralised authority but each group chose the strongest man as their leader, five large eggs appeared on a mountain called Condorcoto. In one of these was the god Pariacaca.

'Huathiacuri was a poor Indian dressed in rags. He was the son of Pariacaca and learnt many arts from his father. In the area there was a rich and powerful Indian, who made himself out to be very wise and to be the creator-god. His house was roofed

Above. Mochica stirrup jar painted with two rearing dragon figures apparently derived from the iguana, a large arboreal lizard whose flesh was valued as food. The presence of cactus leaves seems to indicate that these mythological figures were believed to inhabit the dry coastal deserts. Museum Rietberg, Zurich.

Opposite. Mochica stirrup jar modelled in the form of a fox head. The presence of human attributes such as ear-plugs and headband together with the staring human eyes may indicate that this was intended not as mere decoration but as a personification or 'fox-spirit'. Museum Rietberg, Zurich.

98

with yellow and red birds' feathers and he had a great number of coloured llamas so that it was unnecessary to dye the wool they produced. This rich man fell ill with a foul disease. As Huathiacuri was travelling towards the sea he overheard a conversation between two foxes and learned the cause of the great man's illness: his wife had committed adultery and two serpents were hovering over his house eating his life away, while a two-headed toad was hiding under the grinding stone. Huathiacuri caused the wife to confess, the monsters were destroyed, Tamtanamka recovered and Huathiacuri married the daughter.

'From the five eggs on Mt Condorcoto came forth five falcons, who turned into men. They were Pariacaca and his brothers. They went about doing many marvellous things. Among others, Pariacaca raised a storm and flood which destroyed Tamtanamka and his family.

'Pariacaca decided to try his strength against the rival god Huallallo Caruincho, and went in search of him. Pariacaca's strength lay in wind and rain and flood, Caruincho's in fire. Passing through a village called Huagaihusa in the guise of a poor man, he was not well received

except by one young woman who brought him *chicha* to drink. He therefore destroyed the place by rain and flood, having first warned the woman and her family so that they escaped the disaster. He defeated Huallallo Caruincho and caused him to flee towards the Amazonian forest.

'But Caruincho only pretended to enter the forest. He turned himself into a bird and hid on a cliff of Mt Tacilluka. This time the five sons of Pariacaca swept the mountain with a storm and thunderbolts and Caruincho had to flee again, but he left behind an enormous serpent with two heads. This was changed to stone by Pariacaca. Closely pursued, Caruincho this time took refuge in the jungle. The sons of Pariacaca returned to Mt Llamallaku, where they called together all the peoples and established the cult of Pariacaca. Long afterwards when the Inca came to power they took over this cult and fostered it.'

The loves of Coniraya and Cavillaca
'There was a very ancient *huaca* called Coniraya, but whether his worship preceded or was more recent than that of Pariacaca is not known. He was worshipped under the name of Viracocha up to the time of the Spaniards.

'Coniraya Virachocha came to earth as a poor man dressed in rags and was held in contempt by all. He was the creator of all things and he was responsible for the system of agricultural terracing and irrigation. Coniraya fell in love with a beautiful goddess Cavillaca, who lived as a virgin. One day Cavillaca was sitting under a *lucma* tree and Coniraya turned himself into a beautiful bird and made some of his sperm into the likeness of a *lucma* fruit, which was eaten by Cavillaca. Of this she became pregnant while still a virgin. When the child was a year old she called an assembly of the principal *huacas* of the land to find who was its father. They all turned up in their best clothes, but none admitted the paternity of the child. She therefore let the child free, declaring that the man to whom it would crawl was the father. The child crawled to Coniraya, who sat in rags in the lowest seat. [This myth, the identification by an infant of its divine father, is found in the Chaco and among some tribes of the tropical forest.] Shamed and angered at having been made pregnant by so poor a creature, Cavillaca fled with the child to the sea coast at Pachacamac and there, entering the sea, she and the child became rocks.

'She was followed by Coniraya, who enquired for news of her flight from the various animals he met on his way. He met a condor, who told him she was near and he would soon catch up with her. He therefore blessed the condor and gave it power to fly over mountains and ravines, to build its nest where it would not be disturbed, and to eat all things dead or neglected by their owners, and he gave it immunity. Then he met a fox, who told him that the goddess was far off and he would pursue her in vain. So he cursed the fox and caused it to emit a bad smell and be persecuted and disliked by all men. [According to Rigoberto Paredes the fox is still an animal of ill omen among the Indians of the Altiplano]. Next the lion told him that if he made haste he would soon overtake Cavillaca. So he blessed the lion, saying: "You shall be respected and feared by all and I assign to you the office of punisher and executioner of evil doers. You may eat the llamas of sinners, and after your death you shall still be honoured; for when they kill you and take your skin they shall do so without cutting off the head, which they shall preserve with the teeth, and eyes shall be put in the sockets so as to appear to be still alive. Your feet shall remain hanging from the skin with the tail, and above all those who kill you shall wear your head over their own and your skin shall cover them. This shall they do at their principal festivals so that you shall receive honour from them. I further decree that he who would adorn himself with your skin must kill a llama on the occasion and then dance and sing with you on his back." [This is one of the very few passages bearing on the place of the feline in coastal ritual. There is a comparison with customs reported from Mojos and Chiquitos in the eastern lowlands of Bolivia.] He then met a falcon, who was also blessed. Lastly, parrots gave him bad news, and they were cursed, given loud voices which would put them in danger when feeding and were made hateful to all people.

'When he came to the coast Coniraya found that Cavillaca and her son were turned into stone. He met the two daughters of Pachacamac, who were guarded by a snake. Their mother, Urpi-huachac, was away visiting Cavillaca. Coniraya had intercourse with the elder daughter and wished to do the same with the other, but she turned into a pigeon and flew away. At that time there were no fishes in the sea but Urpi-huachac kept a few in a pond. Angry at her absence, Coniraya emptied them into the sea and from them all the fish in the sea have been born.'

Coniraya and Huayna Capac

'Coniraya went to Cuzco and took Huayna Capac [an Inca monarch] to Lake Titicaca. There he persuaded the king to send a commission to the lowlands of the west. The commission consisted of descendants of the condor, the falcon and the swallow. After five days one of the descendants of the swallow reached his journey's end. There he was given a coffer with instructions that it was to be opened only by the Inca in person. On the outskirts of Cuzco he could contain his curiosity no longer. On taking off the lid he was greatly surprised to see inside a radiantly beautiful woman with hair like gold and dressed as a queen. The vision lasted only an

instant before disappearing. When he reached Titicaca the Inca spared his life because he was descended from the swallow and sent him back to the lowlands. This time he brought the coffer intact into the hands of the Inca, but before the latter could open it Coniraya said to him: "Inca, we must both leave this world. I go to this other world and you shall go to another in the company of my sister. We shall not see each other again." When the coffer was opened an immediate splendour covered the world. The Inca determined not to return to Cuzco. "Here I will stay with my princess," he said, and sent back one of his relations to Cuzco in his place with the command: "Go thou to Cuzco and say that you are Huayna Capac." In that moment the Inca disappeared with his spouse, as did Coniraya.'

Deluge Myths of the Coast

'In the province of Quito there is a district called Cañaribamba and the Indians are called Cañaris from the name of the country. These Indians say that at the time of the deluge two brothers escaped on a very high mountain peak there called Huacay-ñan. According to the fable, as the waters rose the mountain kept increasing in height so that the water could not reach them. When the deluge was over, since the foodstuffs which they had gathered there were finished, they sallied forth over the mountains and valleys seeking food and they built a tiny hut in which they lived, supporting themselves on roots and herbs and suffering much from hunger and fatigue.

'One day, when they had been out to search for food, they returned to their hut and found there a meal prepared to eat and *chicha* to drink [a fermented drink brewed from maize, which is still the 'beer' of the country]. They did not know where it came from or who had prepared it and brought it there. This happened for about ten days, at the end of which they discussed together how to find out who was their benefactor in such great necessity. So the elder of the two remained hidden in the hut and saw two birds arrive of the kind called *aguaque* or *torito*, or in our tongue macaws. They came dressed like Cañaris, with long hair fastened in front as they now wear it. When they came to the hut the Indian in hiding saw the larger of the two take off her *lliclla* (which is the cloak the Indians wear) and begin to cook the food they had brought. When he saw they were beautiful and that they had the faces of women he came out of his hiding place and threw himself upon them. But when they saw the Indian they flew away in anger without leaving anything to eat that day. When the younger brother returned from the country, where he had been looking for food, and found nothing ready and prepared as on previous days he asked his brother the reason and the latter told him what had happened. So the younger brother determined to remain in hiding to see whether the birds returned.

'After three days the macaws returned and began to cook. When he saw that the time was ripe, after they had finished preparing the meal, he leapt to the door and closed it, shutting them inside the hut. The birds became very angry and while he grasped the smaller one the larger flew away. And they say that he had carnal relations with this smaller one and in due course begot by it six sons and daughters. They lived together for a long time on that mountain, supporting themselves on grain which they sowed, the seeds being brought by the macaw. They say that from these six sons and daughters born of the macaw, all the Cañaris are descended, and therefore they regard that mountain as a *huaca* and pay much veneration to the macaw,

whose feathers they value highly for their festivals.

'In the country of Ancasmarca, which is five leagues from Cuzco in the province of Antisuyu, they have the following myth.

'A month before the coming of the deluge their sheep [i.e. llamas: there were no sheep before the Conquest] appeared very sad. They ate nothing during the day and all night long they gazed at the stars, until at last the shepherd in charge of them asked them what they were looking at. They replied that they were looking at the conjunction of the stars, which portended that the world was to be destroyed by water. When he heard this the shepherd consulted with his six sons and daughters and agreed with

them that they should assemble all the food and livestock they could and go to the top of a high mountain called Ancasmarca. They say that as the waters kept on rising and covering the earth, the mountain kept getting higher, so that they never covered it. Afterwards, when the floods receded, the mountain also grew lower. And from those six children of the shepherd who escaped, the province of Cuyos was peopled again.

'These and similar follies they used to tell and still tell.' Cristóbal de Molina of Cuzco: *The Fables and Rites of the Yncas.*

For deluge myths in the Inca cycle see pp. 47 54.

A Creation Myth from the Coast
'They say that at the beginning of the world there came from the north a man called Con, who was without bones. [Probably a supreme deity of pre-Inca mythology who was incorporated into the Inca pantheon.] He was quick and agile and journeyed far. He eased his path by lowering the mountains and raising the valleys simply by the power of his will and word, as became the child of the Sun, which he declared himself to be. He

filled the land with men and women whom he created, and gave them much fruit and bread and the other necessities of life. Nevertheless, because some of them caused him annoyance, he turned the good land he had given them into dry and barren deserts, like those that are by the coast, and caused the rain to cease so that from that time it has not rained in those parts. He left them only the rivers in his clemency that they might support themselves by irrigation and toil.

'There next came Pachacamac (which means Creator), also son of

the Sun and Moon, and he drove out Con and changed his men into monkeys, after which he created anew the men and women who exist today and furnished them with all things they have. In gratitude for such benefits, they made him their god and used to worship him at Pachacamac until such time as the Christians came and cast him out of there, whereat they were much astonished. The temple of Pachacamac near Lima was most celebrated in those lands and was much frequented for worship and for its oracles, for the devil would appear and used to converse with the priests who lived there. The Spanish who went there with Hernando Pizarro after the capture of Atabaliba [Spanicised form of Atahuallpa, the last of the Inca monarchs] robbed it of all its gold and silver and then brought to an end the visions and oracles with the coming of the cross, something which caused the Indians considerable horror and alarm.

Left. One of the statues standing before the small rectangular temples built of roughly hewn stone slabs in the highland district of Huila, around San Agustin. Apart from these figures, Colombia has rather little of interest in the way of prehistoric architecture or stone sculpture. However, the rude but powerfully expressive vigour of these statues has made an enormous impact on modern observers. Often carved in the round, they are squat and powerful, square cut and formidable. They have round, staring and deep-set eyes, broad strong noses with wide nostrils and prominent feline fangs. They wear a loin cloth or a girdle and usually carry a mace or other object. American Museum of Natural History, New York.

Opposite. Mochica stirrup vase in the form of a seated figure with the head or mask of a falcon and playing a skin drum. Despite the lively realism for which the Mochica ceramics are prized in all museums and private collections, it is not possible to obtain from them exact knowledge of beliefs and ritual. Kemper Collection.

Below. A stealite cup of the Cupisnique (coastal Chavín) culture. It bears a carving of two were-jaguars each holding a snake-like body which loops across the base. Dumbarton Oaks, Washington D.C. Robert Woods Bliss Collection.

'They say too that it rained so long a time that all the lowlands were submerged and all men were drowned except those who took refuge in caves high in the mountains whose narrow entries they blocked so that the water could not get in. Inside they stored many provisions and animals. When they no longer heard the rain they sent out two dogs, and as they came back clean but wet they knew that the waters had not subsided. They then sent out more dogs, and when these came back covered with dried mud they knew that the flood had ended and came forth to people the earth. Their greatest trouble and nuisance was caused by the snakes which had been bred by the wetness and slime of the deluge, but at length they killed them and were able to live in safety.

'They also believe in the end of the world. But they think it will be preceded by a great drought and that the Sun and Moon, which they worship, will be lost. And for that reason they howl and weep when there is an eclipse, especially an eclipse of the sun, thinking they are about to lose it and that this will be the end of themselves and the world.' Francisco López de Gomara: *Historia General de las Indias*, Ch. 122.

Marginal, Forest and Southern Andean Peoples

The Chibcha

The Chibcha territory lay in the upper valleys of the rivers Suárez and Chicamocha in what is now Colombia and consisted of three states, the southernmost of which was ruled by the Zipa; to the north was a state ruled by the Zaque, and the smaller realm of the Iraca lay beyond this. The Chibcha had a socio-political organisation more advanced than anything in South America other than the Inca empire and possibly the earlier coastal kingdoms of Peru. But their religion and mythology appear to have been little systematised and were far less adequately reported than those of the Inca.

The creation

In the beginning the world was in darkness and the light was shut up within a being called Chiminigagua, who was the creator of all things that are. The beginning of creation was the shining forth of the light he held inside him. He first created large black birds, which flew over the mountain peaks breathing forth light. Chiminigagua played an unimportant part in the cult and this, according to Pedro Simón in *Noticias historiales de las conquistas de tierra*, was explained by them as being because the Sun (Zuhé) and the Moon (Chía) were more beautiful and therefore more deserving of worship.

The origin of mankind is connected with the goddess Bachúe ('she of the large breasts') or Fura-chogue ('the beneficent female'). Shortly after the origin of light and the creation of the world there emerged from a mountain lake the goddess Bachúe with a three-year-old child. She went with him to the nearby village of Iguaque, north-east of Tunja, the capital of Zaque, and there she brought up the child. Years later when he came to maturity she married him and bore him four to six children at each birth. These and their offspring populated the land. After many generations Bachúe and her husband decided to leave the village. They retired to the mountains and, after exhorting the people to live together in peace and instructing them in the arts of civilisation and social organisation, they re-entered the sacred lake as snakes. Bachúe was worshipped as a protector of agriculture and images of her and her child-husband were the objects of a cult.

A variant myth of the origin of mankind states that the first men were the cacique of Iraca and his nephew the cacique of Ramiquiri who lived when the world was still dark before the creation of light. Bored by the lack of other human beings in the world, they made small statues of yellow clay, which became men, and they cut figures from the stalks of *keck*, which became women. And from these descended the Chibcha peoples. As the world was still dark Ramiquiri, on the orders of Iraca, went up into the sky and turned himself into the Sun. Then Iraca followed him and became the Moon.

Bochica

Bochica was recognised as the chief of the gods. Though invisible, he was worshipped under the image of the Sun, Zuhé or Xué ('Lord'). In addition, he was sometimes identified with the culture hero Nemterequeteba or Chimizapagua.

A gold pectoral of the Chibcha culture showing a figure wearing a fan-shaped headdress. Musée de l'Homme, Paris.

Chibchacum or Chicchechum, patron deity of the labourers and merchants, grew angry against the people of the Bogotá plateau and sent a deluge which flooded the land. In their distress they appealed to Bochica, who showed himself in the rainbow near the town of Soacha and sent the sun to dry the waters. With his staff he struck the rocks and opened a deep chasm through which the flood-waters receded. The great waterfall Tequendama was formed at this time and is a memorial of the event. Chibchacum went underground and since that time he has supported the world on his shoulders; before that the world had been supported on strong pillars in Lake Guayacán. When Chibchacum gets tired and changes his burden from one shoulder to the other he is often careless and that is the cause of earthquakes.

The Culture Hero

Nemterequeteba (sometimes identified with Bochica or the Sun) was a culture hero who came to the country of the Chibcha from the plains of Venezuela to the east. He came twenty ages of seventy years each before the Spanish Conquest. One tradition claims that he entered in the Iraca region, another that he came to the Bacatá region at Pasca in the south. He traversed the Zipa country and then by Muequetá to Cota, where he lived in a cave and had to be protected by a parapet from the large crowds who flocked to hear his preaching. From there he went north to Guane, south through Tunja and east to Gameza and Sugamixi, where he organised a cult, appointed a high priest and then disappeared from view. He was represented as an old man with long hair and a beard down to his girdle. He taught chastity, sobriety, good social order and the arts of spinning, weaving and painting textiles.

Nemterequeteba was also called Sugumonxe or Sugunsúa (the person who disappears) and Chimizapagua (the messenger of Chiminigagua), though records indicate some doubt whether these were two culture heroes or one.

Huitaca

Huitaca was the goddess of indulgence, drunkenness and licence. In myth she was described as a beautiful woman who came after Nemterequeteba and whose teachings were the opposite of his. She was sometimes represented as the wife of Bochica, sometimes as the Moon (Chía), wife of the Sun. Some versions of her myth tell how she was converted by Bochica (or by Chiminigagua or by Nemterequeteba) either into an owl or into the Moon.

The after-life

The Chibcha believed that the soul leaves the body at death and travels to the kingdom of the dead at the centre of the earth through gorges of yellow and black soil. As in some other mythologies, the souls have to first cross a wide river to reach the underworld – in this case they ford the river in boats made from spiders' webs. In the other world each district has its own place and every person upon entering the world of the dead finds a site ready for him to cultivate.

Divine Kingship

The Chibcha tradition also contained a number of myths which, like the myths of Inca origins, supported the institution of divine kingship and connected the dynasties with the gods. The following are examples.

When Nemterequeteba (or Bochica) came to Sugamixi, Nompanem was Iraca. He received Bochica with honour and Bochica dictated the laws, founded the ritual, taught a way of life and introduced the industrial arts. He was succeeded by Firavitoba, husband of his sister. In his time reigned the High Priest Idacanzas, who originated the priestly dynasty.

Hunsahua was the most powerful chief of Tunja, uniting it with Ramiquiri and founding the dynasty of the Zaque. He fell in love with his own sister. The mother refused to countenance the match and therefore the two fled to Chipatae and lived as husband and wife. They returned to the maternal home and the mother in indignation attacked her daughter with the stick for stirring *chicha*. The girl avoided the blow. The measure of *chicha* was upset and formed a lake north of the city of Tunja. The two lovers then left for the south, where at Susa their child was born. The child was turned to stone. The parents in despair wandered southwards until they came to the waterfall

Tequendama on the frontier. Here they determined to settle, but were themselves turned to stone in the middle of the river.

Lake Guatavita was the site of a famous temple. It was said that the deity who inhabited the lake used from time to time to come to the surface in the form of a serpent to receive the offerings brought to the shrine. A certain chief of Guatavita discovered his favourite wife was unfaithful. He had her lover impaled and caused her to eat his private parts. He had songs sung publicly about the matter in order to shame her. Overcome by shame, she threw herself with her infant daughter into the lake. The chief, who was still fond of her, ordered the principal magician to bring mother and daughter back from the lake. The chief magician made a ritual sacrifice, threw heated stones in the lake and dived in after them. He then returned and told the cacique that he had found his wife and the child alive at the bottom of the lake living in an enchanted palace and tending the dragon. He was sent back again to bring them up and returned with the little girl, dead and blind. The dragon had eaten out her eyes. The supposed custom of throwing the lavish offerings of gold into the lake led in time to its identification with the El Dorado of legend.

The Araucanians
The Araucanians of Chile are renowned for having put up the most obstinate resistance first to Inca and later to Spanish domination. Their folklore and legend were influenced both by Inca (perhaps also by pre-Inca) tradition and by Christian teaching. It is virtually impossible to determine what part of the reported mythology belongs to the original strata of belief. *Mitos y Supersticiones*, by Julio Vicuña Cifuentes, a collection gathered from oral tradition, consists almost entirely of folk stories centred for the most part on magic and superstition.

The Araucanians believed in a Supreme Being called Guinechén ('master of the land'), who controlled the forces of nature and gave life to hu-

mans and animals. There was also a cult of Pillan, to whom were attributed natural catastrophes such as storms, floods, volcanic eruptions, and perhaps epidemics and the care of crops. The forces of evil, impersonal and personal, under the name Guecufü, were the subject of elaborate deterrent magical practices. Of this deity Alfred Métraux says (*Handbook of South American Indians*, Vol. 5, p. 561): 'Unfortunately, it is impossible to decide whether this conception of a High God was pre-European or came of the Araucanians' long contact with white people. Our knowledge about this Supreme God's cult does not go back further than 150 years. The many close anal-

ogies between Araucanian beliefs and customs and those of the people of Peru suggests the early existence of a figure of a Creator and Culture Hero who, in the course of years, was refashioned into a Supreme Being, probably under Christian influence.'

Myth of the Deluge
Many centuries ago there was a deluge. The people took refuge from the rising waters on a high peak called Tenten, the animals assembled on another peak, Caicai. The flood was caused by the evil power Guecufü. But in order to frustrate him, the higher waters rose the higher Guinechén raised the mountains. Those who survived the flood were the

ancestors of the Araucanians. According to another version the flood was caused by strife between two serpents, Tenten and Caicai, and the higher Caicai raised the waters, the higher Tenten raised the mountains thus saving the people and animals from drowning. The human beings who had taken refuge on one of the two mountains were then transformed into animals, fishes, birds, and so forth.

Mythical animals

As with many South American peoples, Araucanian folklore is rich in mythical animals. Being a coastal people, they have many aquatic or amphibian creatures among them.

The following are some of the beliefs recorded by Vicuña Cifuentes:

The *Cuero* is a cuttlefish with the appearance of a stretched ox-hide. It has eyes round the edges and four larger eyes in the head. It is enormously strong and when man or animal enters the water, it will rise to the surface, seize and devour them. In parts of Chile it is called Manta. The Trelquehuecuve is a Cuero whose tentacles end in hooves. It will sun itself on the banks of rivers and will seize and squeeze to death anything that comes within its reach. The Huecú is a cuttlefish that lives in deep and solitary lakes and has the form of a brown and black spotted goat-skin. When the water boils and bubbles

over, this is a sign of its presence. It rises to the surface, drags down any bathers it finds and devours them.

The *Guirivilo* or *Negúruvilu* is a long-tailed river fox, or a cross between a fox and a snake, which will seize men or animals in its tail, drag them to the bottom and there drink their blood.

The *Huallepén* is a strong and ill-tempered amphibian animal with the head of a calf and the body of a sheep. It will cover cows and sheep and beget offspring of the same species as the mother but with twisted feet and a twisted muzzle. If a pregnant woman sees a Huallepén or its offspring, or hears its bellow, or dreams of it three nights in succession, she will bear a deformed child.

The *Camahueto* is a gigantic seahorse with strong claws and sharp teeth. It attacks and destroys ships and can open up deep clefts in the shore. It is capable of great speed and when sorcerers visit each other they sometimes travel on its back.

The *Bull of Lake Honda*. Long ago there lived in lake Honda in the province of Linares, a very beautiful bull with horns of gold. It would suck the blood of any living thing that entered the lake, but would leave the lake only to cover the cows of the farm. One day the owner of the farm lost it at a game of dice. The bull was so annoyed at this that it enveloped itself in a thick mist and left the lake followed by all the cows. They hurled themselves into the river Longavi, causing it to overflow and ruin the harvests. With the departure of the bull the lake dried up and filled up again only with water brought by a mule, which still inhabits it.

Serena. Once upon a time there lived an old lady with her daughter. Once when the old lady was ill the daughter wished to go alone to bathe

Characteristically stylised mask in red ceramic from the Chibcha Indians of Guatavita in Colombia. The general shape has affinities with a common Mexican and Central American style. But the rectilinear type of pattern and the stylisation is typical of the regions north of Peru. Musée de l'Homme, Paris.

in the river and when her mother tried to prevent her she struck her in the face. The waters of the river rose and carried the girl down to the sea. When the frantic mother came to look for her some fisherman told her they had seen a strange monster, half woman half fish, being carried to the sea despite her struggles. Now, when fishermen see this monster they take in their nets, either for fear that she will fall into them and break them or else because they know that the fish abandon the waters where she appears. The Serena is also seen in lakes and rivers in the form of a beautiful girl holding up a mirror and combing her hair. Some say that whoever sees the Serena lives but a short life.

Sapo Fuerzo. The Sapo Fuerzo differs from other toads in that it has a shell like a turtle on its back and shines in the dark like a glow-worm. The only way to kill it is to burn it to ashes. There is power in its glance to attract or to repel whatever comes within its reach.

Chonchon. The Chonchon or Chuncho has the form of a human head with very long ears which it uses as wings to fly on dark nights round the houses of the sick. Some believe that its cry is the sign of death. Others say that it wrestles with the 'soul' of the sick man and if it conquers, enters his body and sucks his blood. Some believe that the Chonchon is a sorcerer, others that it is a disguise assumed by the sorcerers. Some believe that when a person has learned the secret of flying from the sorcerers, the head may leave the body at night and fly around as a Chonchon. Husbands tell how in the night they have woken up to find the body of their wives without a head.

Alicanto. The Alicanto is a bird which flies around deposits of gold and silver. It eats the metal and then gives off a brilliant light but becomes too heavy to fly. It is difficult to catch because it turns off its light when pursued and disappears in the darkness; or it may lead its pursuers to a precipice which, unseen in the darkness of night, causes their death. The Alicanto is sometimes confused with the *Carbunco,* an animal with a double shell which can open and shut. When open it gives forth a brilliant light from the gold it has inside. The Carbunco lives in the mountains but comes down at night for water. Some say it has the shape of an ear of maize and many legs.

Tales of mythical animals are very common throughout South America. Oblitas Poblete tells of the belief among the highland Indians of Bolivia in the *Qate-Qate,* or Uma-khawa, which has the shape of a human head and flies about by night making a noise like a rusty door-hinge. It pursues murderers and criminals in the form of divine justice or the remorse of conscience. The *Lari-Lari,* or Jinchuqqaño, is a little bird which flies by night and can change itself into a cat, dog, monkey, etc. Its song is sweet and seductive and those who hear it are overcome by the desire to sleep. Those who succumb are doomed, for the Lari-Lari enters their body and steals their soul, causing a mortal disease. There are many stories of seductive maidens and other appearances which cause the death of unwary travellers. The *Pilulo* is a handsome young man who attracts women to their doom, leading them over rough and pathless country which seems to them like beautiful flowery meadows and abandons them in the wilds. Among the Guiana Indians any conspicuous natural features, such as a waterfall or a strangely growing tree, was regarded as the abode of a spirit which might be incarnated as an animal. Many tribes believe in supernatural protectors of fish or game, such as the *Rato* of the Taulipáng and the *Soinidi* of the Toba. These usually have the form of a particularly fine member of the species but are regarded as spirits which can, on occasions, take human

Terracotta figurine with incised decoration and high conical headdress, from the Paracas peninsula. The statue gives some idea of the racial types who inhabited the southern and central coast of Peru about 500 B.C. At that time the Paracas people were making some of the finest pottery and textiles ever produced in South America. Kemper Collection.

form. They are akin to the ancestral spirits of the family or tribe. In Tierra del Fuego the constellations are believed to be incarnations of such spirits which have migrated into the sky.

The Peoples of the Far South

The habitat of the Yahgan is the mountainous archipelago of Tierra del Fuego, which is the most southerly tip of the Andean mountain chains. They are people of whom Charles Darwin stated that they were lacking any religious concept. Later investigation has shown that they believe in a Supreme Being Watauineiwa ('The Most Ancient One'), called also 'The Powerful, The Most High', and commonly prayed to under the title 'My Father'. He is a benevolent god, who has no body but lives above the heavens. He is not conceived as a creator, but as the giver and sustainer of life. He is the protector of the social and moral code. In rites of mourning complaints are addressed to Watauineiwa for having allowed the person to die. The Alacaluf believe that the Supreme Being Xolas puts the soul into each new-born baby and that on a man's death his soul is reabsorbed by Xolas. The Yahgan believe that on death the spirits of the dead (koshpik) fly away to the east. Watauineiwa features importantly in initiation ceremonies but is not the centre of a cycle of myth.

The cosmological mythology includes a deluge and a culture hero. The origin of civilisation is explained by the myth of two brothers, Yoalox, and their sister. The elder brother was stupid and the younger brother, the cutlure hero, was clever. The myth functions importantly during the initiation ceremony, called ciexaus.

The Yahgan have no cult of ancestors but a certain fear of the dead, and their kina rite has analogies with ghost rituals of other tribes such as the Alacaluf. Women are excluded from the kina rituals and an elaborate myth is told in explanation of this practice, envisaging an earlier time when the women were the masters and in order to maintain their supremacy wore spirit masks which hoodwinked the men. The myth tells how the deception was discovered and all the women killed except one young child. In the ceremonies the men wear elaborate spirit masks and threaten the women with penalties if they are not submissive.

The Ona, who inhabit Tierra del Fuego, believe in a Supreme Being Temaukel, who is without body, wife or children, who has always existed and sustains the universe and the socio-moral code. He lives above the stars, is invisible, benevolent and the recipient of individual prayers in time of trouble. Souls (kaspi) go to the place of Temaukel after death.

The first man, Kenos, was the agent of Temaukel in bringing civilisation and culture to mankind. The myth also tells of the early ancestors of the Ona, who turned into rivers, mountains and lakes; of a hunter-hero Kwanyip who overcame the spirit of evil, Chenuke, and who waged perpetual war against a giant black and invisible cannibal who ranged the hills. The Ona initiation rite kloketen, like the Yahgan kina exclusively for men, was associated with a myth featuring the conquest of superiority by the men after a period when women were dominant. The myth is in the form of a victory of the sun over the moon.

No mythology of origins is recorded of the Chono and Alacaluf of southern Chile and information from the Tehuelcho and Puelcho tribes of the Patagonian pampas is very sparse. Among the Puelcho the Sun and Moon were brothers. The Sun, the elder of the two, was the intelligent one and beneficent to man. They believed in a Supreme Being, whose name has been very variously reported, and in a supreme spirit of evil sometimes called Ellal. Their mythology is said to have included a story of a flood, after which the world was populated by men issuing from mountain caves. The Tehuelcho had a Supreme Being, sometimes reported by the name Guayavacuni, and a good spirit, who may or may not have been identified with him and who created the tribes of men at a hill called God's Hill and dispersed them from there. Alternatively Heller, son of the Sun, is reported as creator of men and bringer of civilisation.

Brazil

The mythology and folklore of Brazil, a Portuguese-speaking country, is a unique compound of Portuguese-Christian, African and Forest Indian elements. Of African origin are many myths and legends connected with magical rites and cults imported by the slave-workers and sometimes amalgamated with indigenous magical beliefs under the name 'Catimbo.' Catimbo has its ritual days devoted to the powers of Good or the powers of Evil. Most widely disseminated is the mythology of indigenous origin, which has much in common with the mythology of the Forest Indians elsewhere in South America although there are distinctive features of interest.

Among the most prominent beliefs are the following:

The Jurupari, represented in early Catholic literature as a Devil, was in fact worshipped as a divine protector of family morality and tribal custom, inflicting condign punishment for infringements. The cult still survives in the Mato Grosso region.

The Caipora is queen and protector of forest animals, respected and feared by the Indians. She rides the forest on a peccary, smoking a clay pipe with a sprig of sarsaparilla in her hand, and can bring back to life animals slain by the hunters. She can plague with continuing bad luck those who fall out of her favour. She is recognised by a piercing whistle.

The Anhanga is a supernatural stag which protects the animals of the plains as the Caipora protects those of the forests. He can change hunted animals into a phantom which leads the pursuers into wild and desolate places where they perish of hunger.

The Curupira is a supernatural being who lives by lonely forest streams and protects the trees from useless destruction. He has the form of a restless little Indian with green teeth who walks backwards in order to mislead. He was formerly believed to be a plague of the fishermen and rubber workers.

In Museum catalogues these crude figures of the Forest Indians of Brazil are commonly labelled 'demon' or 'devil.' In fact they existed between mythological figures and personifications of types, combining the attributes of both. Staatliche Museum Für Volkerkunde, Munich. *Left.* Mask of a forest spirit. *Above.* Mask of a fish demon. *Opposite.* Jaguar demon. *Below left.* Tapir demon.

The *Boiuna* is the Great Serpent Goddess who dominates the rivers of the Amazon. Her eyes shine in the dark like lanterns. Fierce and insatiable she searches the rivers at night for living flesh and she can impregnate women by her mere presence or turn herself into a phantom ship. She is destructive and implacable.

The myth of the *Lobishomen* or Werewolf is very widely spread and may be of European origin. Certainly many of the details of the belief have been captured from European superstition and amalgamated. The Lobishomen roves through the night pursued by the barking of dogs, attacks and murders unaccompanied travellers or else turns them into werewolves.

The Tupari

In 1948 a young Swiss ethnologist, Franz Caspar, visited the Tupari Indians, a primitive tribe who had virtually no previous contacts with white people, living along the Rio Branco in the Mato Grosso region of Brazil, and remained with them for four months as a guest-member of the tribe. The author, who had known him in La Paz, happened to be in Guayaramerín on the Rio Mamoré when he came out, and travelled with him overland to Cachuela Esperanza. In his book *Tupari* Caspar has given a brief account of what he learnt, despite severe linguistic difficulties which attended the exchange of ideas on other than practical matters, about their beliefs concerning the spirits of heaven and the origins of man and concerning the souls of the dead. The importance assigned to magicians is common to almost all the native peoples of South America and has to a considerable extent survived Christianisation.

The Spirits of Heaven

Once upon a time no men were yet on earth and no *kiad-pod* in heaven. There was only a big block of rock, beautiful and smooth and shining. Now this block of stone was a woman. One day it split and brought forth a man amid streams of blood. This was Valedjád. And again the rock split and brought forth a second man. His name was Vab. Both were magicians. But they had no wives, so they made themselves stone axes and cut down two trees. They then killed an agouti, took out its front teeth and from them each carved himself a woman.

Thus too did the other primitive magicians arise — the *vamoa-pod*, from water and from the earth.

Valedjád was a wicked magician. He very often grew angry and whenever he did so it rained. So he flooded the whole land and many *vamoa-pod* perished. The survivors racked their brains to think how they could rid themselves of Valedjád. One of the primitive magicians, Arkoanyó, hid in a tree and poured liquid beeswax on Valedjád as he went past. This sealed up his eyes, nostrils and fingers so that he could do no more mischief. And then they wanted to remove him far, far away. Many birds tried to pick him up and carry him off. But they were all too small. At last they found a large bird which was strong enough. He seized Valedjád and flew with him far away to the north. There he put him down and there to this

day Valedjád lives in a stone hut. And when he becomes angry we have rain here.

Another evil magician was called Aunyain-á. He had great tusks like a boar and used to eat the children of his neighbours. These neighbours at last decided to escape from this monster and leave the earth. One day Aunyain-á went into the forest to shoot a mutum fowl and while he was away they climbed up a creeper which hung from the sky down to the earth. At that time the sky was not as far up as it is today, but hung down quite near the earth.

When Aunyain-á came back from the hunt he could no longer find his neighbours. He asked a parrot where they had gone. The parrot sent him

119

to the river, but Aunyain-á found no traces in the sand. Then the parrot laughed him to scorn and said that all his neighbours had climbed up into the sky. Aunyain-á grew furious and tried to shoot the parrot, but he did not hit him.

Then Aunyain-á seized the creeper in order to overtake the fugitives. But the parrot quickly flew up high and began to gnaw through the creeper. Aunyain-á plunged down to the ground and lay there shattered. From his arms and legs there grew caymans and iguanas and from his fingers and toes little lizards of many kinds. The vultures ate the rest of him. Since that time the primitive magicians live up in heaven. A few of them still live on the earth but they live very far away from here.

Many of the *kiad-pod* look like men but they have their peculiarities. One talks through his nose, another has a twisted mouth and a third, Vamoá-togá-togá, has a navel a span long. And none of them has any hair on the back of his head.

But there were some primitive magicians in this heaven who had animal form. There was a sapajou monkey, a black monkey, a howler monkey

and many others. They too were proper magicians, said the Indians.

'They can't talk and sing like men. And when here in the *maloca* [village] the magicians sniff tobacco and *aim-peh*, then the powder also goes up into the noses of those monkeys in heaven: they sneeze and come down from heaven to take part in Vaitó's magic ceremonies.

'Ordinary people cannot see these dwellers in heaven. Only our magicians have dealings with them during the raising of spirits. Then the *kiad-pod* come into the *maloca* and the souls of our magicians go to heaven and wander through the most distant places of the world. There they receive from the spirits mysterious yellow grains, the *pagab*. With the *pagab* the magicians bewitch and kill their enemies.'

The Origins of Man
About their own origins the Tupari said:

'Long ago there were on earth no Tupari or other men. Our ancestors lived under the ground where the sun never shines. They suffered great hunger, for they had nothing to eat but wretched palm fruits. One night they

discovered a hole in the earth and climbed out. This was not far from the tent of the two primeval magicians Aroteh and Tovapod. There they found peanuts and maize. They ate some and next morning they vanished again into the hole between the stones from which they had emerged. This they did night after night. Aroteh and Tovapod believed that it was the agoutis which were stealing their crops, but one morning they saw the tracks of men and found the holes through which they used to creep out. With a long pole they dug about in the hole and prised out the stones. Then men began to stream out in great hordes until the primeval magicians closed up the hole again.

'But the men were ugly to look upon. They had long canine teeth like those of wild boars and between their fingers and toes the flesh was webbed like a duck's. Aroteh and Tovapod snapped off their tusks and shaped their hands and feet. Since then men have no longer had long tusks or webs but beautiful teeth and fingers and toes.

'Many men remained in the earth. They are called *kinno* and still live there. One day, when all the people

Left. A typical mummy bundle from Peru, elaborately tied up with fibre rope. Bodies for burial – the so-called 'mummies' – were carefully wrapped in many layers of cloth with sand between, and the whole was roped into a 'bundle'. Inside it were often placed mortuary gifts of pottery, fine robes, utensils, costume jewellery, toys, and so forth. The bundles have been found buried in extensive cemeteries, preserved by the hot dry atmosphere of the coastal desert. Musée de l'Homme, Paris.

Opposite. Suyá Indians with bundles of timbó which have been crushed and will be used to poison a nearby lake. Later the Indians will return to collect the dead fish floating on the surface.

of the earth have died, the *kinno* will come out of the ground and live here.

'But the men whom Aroteh had let out of the earth did not all find room in the same place. We Tupari remained here, the others wandered far away in all directions. They are our neighbours: the Arikapú, Yabutí, Makuráp, Aruá, and all the other tribes.'

The Souls of the Dead

When a Tupari dies, then the pupils of his eyes leave him and change into a *pabid*. The *pabid* does not walk the earth like living men but his path to the realm of the dead leads over the backs of two great crocodiles and to giant snakes, a male and a female. Ordinary folk cannot see these crocodiles; only the magicians see them in their dreams. Often the snakes rear up towards the sky and when it rains they become visible to everybody; that is the rainbow. The *pabid*, then, strides over the backs of the snakes

Opposite. Man of the Waura tribe preparing special feathers, which he keeps in a rolled fibre mat. These people attached much importance to the various spirits of good and evil, and each tribe or group evolved magical practices to try to control them.

Above. Modern devil mask from Oruro, Bolivia, made from plaster, mirror glass and rubber tubing. The eyes are made from electric light bulbs. The Oruro ceremonies are an annual event and devil masks are still on sale. Horniman Museum, London.

and the crocodiles to the village of the dead. He also passes two huge jaguars who frighten him with their roars, but who cannot do anything to him. At last the dead man reaches his new home, which lies on the big river Mani-mani. But he sees nothing of all this, for his eyes are still closed. He is received by two fat worms, a male and a female. They bore a hole in his belly and eat all his intestines. Then they crawl out again.

Now comes Patobkia, the head magician and chief of the *maloca* of the dead. He sprinkles stinging pepper juice into the newcomer's eyes and now for the first time the *pabid* sees where he has come to. In astonishment he looks about him and sees nothing but strangers. They all have hollow bellies because the worms have eaten their bowels and their teeth are nothing but short stumps. Sadly he asks Patobkia: 'Where am I and who are all these people?' 'These are your parents! These are your brothers and sisters!' laughs Patobkia scornfully. But this is a cruel lie. The *pabid* sees neither parents nor brothers and sisters but only strange beings, staring dully at him. 'Then I really have died and gone to the *pabid*,' says the dead man. And with horror he notices that he too has only short stumps left for teeth and no bowels. Then Patobkia hands him a bowl of *chicha*. The new *pabid* drinks it and Patobkia leads him further into the village of the dead. There an old couple of giant primeval magicians await the newcomer. If he is a man he must in full view of everyone copulate with the ancient giantess Vaugh-'eh, but if the *pabid* is a woman she must give herself to old Mpoká-lero. . . Later the *pabid* no longer have intercourse in the usual human manner but the men breathe on a bundle of leaves and throw it at the backs of the women and in this way they become pregnant and bear children.

The *pabid* live in large, round huts; they have no hammocks but sleep standing up in the huts. They lean against the supporting posts and cover their eyes with their arms. They clear no woods and plant no fields.

Patobkia does all this with a magic gesture of his hand and with his magic breath.

The *chicha* which the *pabid* women brew from peanuts does not ferment, so the dead men cannot get drunk. However, they frequently sing and dance in their full array of feathers, and the Tupari's magicians hear their songs when they visit the *pabids*' village in their dreams. If ever a *pabid* falls ill he eats papaws. The *pabid's* papaws are much bigger and sweeter than those of the living and make sick men well and old men young again.

In addition to the *pabid* the Tupari believe that the dead have a second ghostly existence in the region of the body. Caspar reports as follow:

'When someone dies and the pupils of his eyes go off to the *pabid*, then we bury him in the hut or where we have burnt down an old hut. Immediately the heart begins to grow in the dead man's body and after a few days it is as big as the head of a child. Inside the heart springs up a little man who grows bigger and bigger and bursts open the heart, just as a bird breaks its shell. This is the *ki-apoga-pod*. But he cannot crawl out of the ground and weeps with hunger and thirst. The relatives of the dead man therefore go hunting. When they come back they hold three sessions of snuff-taking with the magicians. The chief magician draws the *ki-apoga-pod* from the ground, cleans him and shapes his face and limbs, for when he comes out of the ground he is still unformed clay. Then the magician gives him something to eat and drink and lets him loose in the air. Up there the *ki-apoga-pod* live.

'But if the dead man was a magician, then his *apoga-pod* does not float away to those distant places but stays in the *maloca*. There the souls of the dead magicians eat our food and drink our *chicha*. Down from the dome of the hut they cast a spell on us at night and produce our dreams. The souls of the dead wives of the magicians also hover up there.'

The Chaco Tribes

The Chaco, said to be derived from a Quechua word meaning 'hunting ground', is a name loosely applied to the large plain which extends from the edge of the Mato Grosso region to the Argentine pampas. The greater part of the territory is now divided between Bolivia and Paraguay. The early mythology of the Chaco tribes is very unevenly reported. Such records as there are point in the direction of a lively, not to say exuberant, fancy but have the appearance rather of a colourful and diversified folklore than any systematised mythology.

The reports of missionaries from the seventeenth century give no clear evidence of belief in a Supreme Being, although the Chamacoco had a supreme goddess who was the mother of all spirits (*guara*), controlled the sun and saw that men had water. The Mocobi had a benevolent spirit Co-taá, invisible in the sky, who made the earth, maintained the sun, moon and stars in their courses and made the earth fruitful. It is, in such cases, particularly difficult to determine how far such attributes reflect missionary teaching or to what extent they belonged to indigenous belief.

The sun, moon and certain constellations were often personified and made the subjects of folk tales. The Pleiades were called 'Grandfather', their annual disappearance being attributed to illness and their reappearance hailed with rejoicing. In some myths of the Pilaga the rainbow was thought to kidnap children and kill people by its tongue. Among most tribes of the Chaco the sun was female and the moon male. The typical story of two brothers, one clever and successful the other stupid and blundering, the sort of story which is found throughout South America, was among the Chamacoco and Mataco told of the Sun and Moon. The Sun was the successful brother and the Moon was his unsuccessful twin. Many stories were told illustrating these qualities.

The thunderbolt – or the lightning – was a hairy old woman who fell to the earth during a storm and could only return to the sky in the smoke of a fire. The rain was produced by a red ant-eater, or by a female spirit called Kasogonaga hanging in the sky, or by thunderbirds from a celestial jar. Eclipses were thought by some to be caused by an attack of the celestial jaguar on the Sun or Moon. The Lule thought that a large bird was hiding the heavenly body with its wings. The Lule attributed all illnesses to a mountain grub of imaginary form called Ayacua, armed with bow and stone-tipped arrows. According to the folklore of several tribes there was once an enormous tree connecting earth with the sky and men used to climb the tree in order to reach the celestial hunting-grounds. The tree was burnt by a vengeful woman, and the men who were caught in the sky were changed into stars.

Creation

Creation stories were no less various and unorganised. The Lengua attributed the creation of the world to a gigantic beetle, which also created the spirits and produced the first man and woman (originally stuck together) from particles of soil he threw away. The Mbaya told that men were hatched from eggs laid by a large bird on the top of a mountain; or they came from a large cave in the north; or they first lived underground and were released by a dog. The Chamacoco said that men lived underground and reached the surface by a rope made from the fibre of a plant named caraguata. The first to come were very tiny. There was little food on the earth to support them, so when a few had come to the surface a dog gnawed through the cord. Later the Chamacoco and other peoples climbed to the sky by an enormous tree trunk and they all fell to earth again. That is why the Chamacoco are now so few. Alternatively the Chamacoco were at first shut up inside a quebracho tree so huge that they could play ball in it. A man came and split the trunk and let them out. According to the Matado and Toba, women came down from the sky by a rope in order to steal the food of the men, who were at that time animals. The rope was cut by a bird and the women had to remain. The Tereno tradition is that two supernatural brothers were hunting birds and came to a deep crevasse; from this hole the Tereno came, shivering with cold and blinded by the sun.

The Destruction of the World and Culture Heroes

There are myths of a deluge, caused by a menstruating girl; a destruction of the world by cold; a destruction by fire caused by the fall of the sun. There are numerous folk tales of the origin of fire. It was the property of the thunderbirds, and men learnt its uses when they tasted snails which had been roasted by the birds. The Chamacoco attributed it to a culture hero Carancho, who had received it from the owl.

The culture hero Carancho, sometimes identified with the hawk, features in the folk myth of several tribes. He is clever and benevolent. In many stories he is accompanied by the stupid or mischievous fox in adventures analogous to the 'two brothers' stories which are a common theme of South American folklore. Other culture heroes were Peritalnik, Asin (a bald, large-bellied warrior who produced food from under his robe), the aquatic bird Nedamik. The figure of the 'trickster' is a common feature; he is a vainglorious, boastful and malicious individual, but easily tricked in his turn. A little man called Kosodot taught men to hunt, his wife Kopilitara for her part taught women the art of pottery, and weaving was learned from the Spider.

Mythical Trees

It is a matter for no surprise that peoples whose ecology was closely linked with the semi-tropical forest had many folk legends of trees, in addition to the mythical trees which connected the earth with the sky. The following are examples.

There is a rare fern or liana called Yobec Mapic which is burned and the ashes used as salt. It is told that the god Cotaá created a miraculous tree which would yield food and drink to the hungry people. The mischievous spirit Neepec tipped over it a pitcher filled with tears and spoiled the taste.

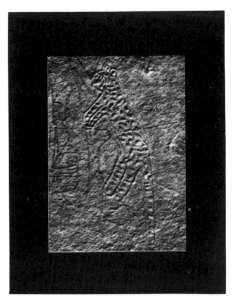

Engraving of a puma from the Atacama desert. Behind it is what may be a demon figure or the figure of a magician, carved on a stone of what is believed to be a cult site of great antiquity.

When the god Cotaá returned and saw what was done, he turned the damage into good and explained that the salty taste might serve for seasoning meat dishes.

There is a large and beautiful tree called Timbo whose crest is like a huge umbrella. Its wood is used for canoes and pirogues. Its fruit is a black berry shaped like an ear, and for this reason the tree is called 'black ear'. The Guaraní say that in the past a famous chief Saguaa had a daughter Tacuareé of whom he was very fond. Tacuareé fell in love with a distant chief of another tribe and left her father to travel through the forest to join her lover. Saguaa set out to follow her and constantly put his ear to the ground in the attempt to hear her steps across the forest. At last, unable to travel any farther, he collapsed in exhaustion and lay with his ear still glued to the ground. The ear put down roots and from them grew the Timbo tree.

The Matacos have a different version. They tell that when the first strangers invaded the territories of the Chaco the daughter of a chieftain, the most beautiful woman in the land, put herself at the head of the repelling forces. Her father remained at home and, overcome by anxiety, constantly put his ear to the ground listening for the sounds of the returning force. But it never did return and the chief at last died with his ear still to the ground. Thence grew the Timbo tree.

The Chane have a story which seems to carry echoes of the Tree of Life theme which was common in the Guianas. In former times there was a huge yuachan tree in which swam fish, which the men of old times used to shoot. They were not allowed to kill the larger ones but the Trickster, true to character, disregarded this prohibition and shot a large dorado. This caused the earth to be flooded. But the Trickster fortunately put an end to the flood by opening up with his spear a passage through which the waters were able to flow into the sea.

The foregoing are samples of material which has been reported in some abundance, together with animal stories and some legends of tribal chieftains. Most of the material is on the borders between folk story and myth. The coexistence of various alternative stories on the same theme has led to the supposition that much of the folklore of the Chaco tribes was imported from other cultural centres – particularly the Aymará and Quechua. This would also account in part for its variety and its fragmentary and unsystematised state.

Above. Panel from a painted textile showing Bochica, the Chibcha sun god. Chibcha culture. Fifteenth century A.D., Colombia.

Opposite. Man of the Karaja tribe wearing a special feather headdress used during a boy's initiation. Crisis rituals played an important part in both personal and social life among the Marginal and Tropical Forest peoples.

Some Riddles of South American Myth

Jaguar Cults

Archaeological evidence tells overwhelmingly in support of a widespread religion based on a feline deity – probably a jaguar or mountain cat – from the Cultist period (c. 850 B.C.) onwards. The feline motif dominated in the Chavín culture and is common on early Paracas textiles. Wendell C. Bennett and Junius Bird in their *Andean Culture History* call the feline design the 'primary symbol of the [Chavín] religion'; and in the later, Experimental Period (c. 400 B.C.) through to the Mastercraftsman Period (c. A.D. 0-900) – in the Nazca and Mochica styles for example – they say that 'the feline is the most universal religious figure represented'. J. Alden Mason in his *Ancient Civilisations of Peru* states that in the Cultist period: 'A religious cult in which a feline deity, puma or jaguar, played the most prominent role was the common element, for otherwise the small villages had no political bond and the local cultural variations from valley to valley were considerable'. G. H. S. Bushnell commits himself to the statement that the frequency of feline features in the carvings 'makes it virtually certain that the jaguar was a very powerful god, perhaps the most powerful of all'. Such is the voice of archaeology. And some of the representations of the jaguar motif make so strong an impact even now that it is difficult not to suppose that they had a profound religious significance. Yet in the absence of written records the supposition of an organised religion featuring a jaguar-god can only remain very speculative.

Some writers have derived the name 'Titicaca' from the Aymará *titi*, a general term for a feline. But this

etymology is hardly more convincing than the derivation, given for example by Garcilaso, from the Quechua word *titi*, which means 'lead'. In the early and classical periods of Tiahuanaco art the head of the puma (South American lion) was a frequent motif. There have been found at Tiahuanaco zoomorphic stone figures, called locally *Chacha-puma* or Lion-man, representing a man with a feline head, often with an expression of exaggerated ferocity. These are usually about three feet high and sometimes carry a cudgel in the right hand and a human head in the left. Examples of these figures may be seen in the Tiahuanaco Museum at La Paz.

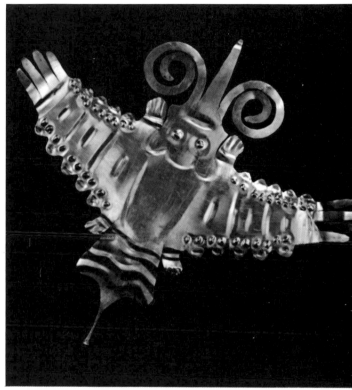

Garcilaso says that the Indians of the Bolivian Altiplano worshipped the tiger and the lion among many other animals during the stage of naturalistic animism, and that if they met one of these animals (or a bear) they would offer no resistance but fall down before it. Cieza de León and Bernal Diez de Casillo mention sacrifical worship of the tiger after the fall of the Inca, the former as far north as Quito. Polo de Ondegardo speaks of forest Indians who worshipped a star called Chuquichinchay, which he says 'is a tiger in whose charge are the tigers, bears and lions'. José de Arriaga states that the Devil appeared to the native sorcerers in the form of a lion or tiger. Guamán Poma de Ayala asserts that in very early times the Yarohuillka had a complete hierarchy based on the puma, and Juan de Betanzos mentions a city which was called 'Body of the Lion' and its inhabitants the members. In his *Descripción biográfica, histórica y estadística de Bolivia* Alcides d'Orbigny described survivals of a tiger cult as late as 1815. To this day in the traditional dances performed at Carnival throughout the Altiplano the tiger mask is prominent.

In eastern Bolivia, where the jaguar is indigenous, men still go out to kill the jaguar single-handed and armed only with a wooden spear in order to win the status of warriors. The archaeologist Leo Pucher reported a belief that such men are believed to have the power to turn themselves into tigers at night. The Chiriguani still believe in a fabulous green tiger Yaguarogui, which causes eclipses of the sun and moon by attempting to eat them, as reported by Dorotéo Giannecchini in *Diccionario Chiriguano-Español*. A ceramic representation of what was believed to be the Yaguarogui was found by Julio Tello at Chavín. The common practice of howling and shouting during an eclipse is sometimes explained as an attempt to scare off the jaguar which is eating the sun.

Among the Mojo and some other peoples of the eastern lowlands of Bolivia the jaguar was regarded with superstitious awe and was the object of a cult. Persons who had been wounded by a jaguar and had escaped with their lives constituted a special class of magicians or shamans called *camacoy*. They warned the people when a jaguar was about to prey on the community and were thought to have supernatural contact with the

Above. Ceramic figure with ceremonial headdress and large ear. plugs, seated on a throne on the base of which are carved jaguars. Royal Scottish Museum, Edinburgh.

Right. Double-spouted Nazca jar painted with a feline figure, depicted with metal facial ornaments, whiskers and fringe covering the lower part of the face and with a metal headband in the centre of which is a stylised face. This may indicate a priest of a Jaguar cult. Museum Rietberg, Zurich.

Opposite. An Indian of the Amazon basin, fully painted. This young man of the Waura tribe is wearing painted hair, feather ear-tassels, and a necklace of jaguar claws. Belief in jaguar spirits – or were-jaguars – was once widely held among the more primitive tribes, and may have been the source of a jaguar cult in the Central Andes.

jaguar spirits. Sometimes they were believed to be able to turn themselves into jaguars. The belongings of persons killed by a jaguar were sacred to the jaguar cult. A hunter who had killed a jaguar acquired great prestige. The secret name of the jaguar was revealed to him by the shamans and was adopted by him as his own. The claws and skull were kept as trophies in the communal drinking hall. But no developed jaguar mythology is recorded from these peoples.

There is no lack of evidence of a superstitious worship of the feline along with the worship of many other animals and natural objects. But there is lacking a tradition of an organised religion of the jaguar or of a feline god such as the archaeologists suppose, and no myth of the jaguar bulks at all important in the recorded mythology. While the mythological records are distressingly fragmentary, such as they are they do not offer support to the interpretations of archaeology which suggest a religious culture based on the worship of a feline deity.

Mythology and Cult of the Dead
Few peoples anywhere in the world have given evidence of so universal a care for the dead as the tribes of the Central Andean region. Methods of

burial varied widely from one place to another. In the highlands the bodies of thc dead were dried in the cold air and kept in the houses or put away in caves; the Inca had an elaborate ceremonial of burial and the mummified bodies of the kings were preserved each in its own shrine and brought forth from time to time in ceremonial procession. By far the greatest part of the art objects and handicrafts which now fill public museums and private collections throughout the world were recovered from the cemeteries of the sandy coastal valleys.

While it is thought to have existed from very early times, the cult of the dead became more elaborate and more highly organised as civilisation progressed. By analogy with what we know about similar practices else-

131

Above. A mummy mask from the Mochica culture, *c.* A.D. 500. The face is made of beaten copper and the eyes of shell. Art Institute of Chicago, Illinois. Gift of Mr and Mrs Nathan Cummings.

Opposite. Figure which may have been used with a mummy bundle, or as a temple or tomb offering. The wooden head and body, thirty-two inches high, was made by the Huacho Indians in the fourteenth century A.D. The cap and headdress are of llama wool, the shawl of cotton and the hair is made from plant fibre. American Museum of Natural History, New York.

Above. Pottery jar from the great adobe frontier fortress of Paramonga on the river Paravilca at the southern extremity of the Chimu kingdom. The fortress may have been built as a defence against the growing power of the highland Inca. The neck of the jar is in the form of a human head naturalistically treated. On the body is relief decoration representing the crowned figure of a priest-king, or possibly a deity, dancing with two felines. Kemper Collection.

where, it is generally presumed that this complex ceremonial care for the dead points towards a well-developed belief in an afterlife. For example, J. Alden Mason says of the Salinar, a people of the Chicama valley in northern Peru from the transition period between the Cultist and Experimental: 'The better care of the dead indicates a belief in the afterlife, and probably early phases of the cult of ancestor worship which later be-

came of maximum cultural importance. The bodies were interred wrapped in or covered with textiles, and provided with pottery vessels and gourds containing food and drink. They wore their ornaments and a piece of beaten gold was often put in the mouth. Dogs were sometimes placed at the feet, together with pieces of chalk, quartz and other stones, generally of a white colour. Red powder (cinnabar?) was found in most graves. The body was almost always laid at full length, on the right side, in elliptical graves covered with great stone slabs.

An elaborate mortuary ritual indicating care for the dead and attention to the needs of the departed in the future life implies a developed mythology of the afterlife. Yet in the recorded mythology the life after death plays so insignificant a part that one can but wonder whether the Indians withheld from the Spanish this most

cherished sector of their beliefs, or whether the Spanish chroniclers were uninterested in eliciting and recording beliefs which differed from the orthodox Christian picture of the afterlife. What has survived on this matter is summed up in the following passage from Cieza de León.

'I have frequently mentioned in this history that in the greater part of this kingdom of Peru it is a custom much practised and cherished by the Indians to bury with the bodies of the dead all their most prized possessions and some of the most beautiful of their women and those most beloved by them. . . From the lofty and magnificent tombs they have made, adorned with tiles and vaulted roofs, from the fact that they place with the dead all their goods and their women and servants, an ample store of provisions

and numerous jars of *chicha* (that is the wine they use), and also their weapons and personal adornments, one can gather that they had understanding of the immortality of the soul and knew that there was more to a man than the mortal body.

'Deceived by the Devil, they accomplished his commands, for he gave them to understand (as they themselves say) that after death they would return to life in another place which he had made ready for them; and there they would eat and drink at their pleasure as they had done before they died. And in order that they might believe what he told them was true and not a lie and deceit, from time to time, when the will of God is served by giving him the power and allowing it, he would take the form of one of the chiefs who was dead

and, showing himself in the chief's true shape and figure with the appearance he bore during life, ornaments, decorations and all, he gave them to believe that this chief lived on in another world, happy and at peace, just as they saw him. Because of these sayings and illusions of the Devil these blind Indians, taking those false

Above. Fragment of painted cotton fabric, showing winged feline figures together with trophy heads and parts of plants. Museum Rietberg, Zurich.

Opposite. Suyá hunter and fisherman from the Xingú river, adorned with a flower headdress to celebrate good fishing. The Indians of the tropical rainforest and the Amazonian area had a culture of their own well adapted to the conditions of their environment. It was thus different in most important essentials from that of the Central Andes.

appearances for reality, give more attention to beautifying their tombs and sepulchres than to anything else. When one of the chiefs dies they bury with him his treasure, his women and youths and other persons whom he held in close friendship while alive. Thus from what I have related it was the general opinion of these Indians of the valleys and even those of the highlands of Peru that the spirits of the dead do not die but live on for ever and that they would all come together again in the other world, and there they believed they would live at ease, eating and drinking, which is their chief delight.' Pedro de Cieza de León; *Crónica del Perú*, Part I, Ch. 62.

The Amazons

The tenacious myth of the Amazon women originated with the historic voyage of Francisco Orellana up the 'river of the Amazons' in 1540, though rumours going back much earlier predisposed the Spanish Conquistadores to the belief. When he returned to Europe Christopher Columbus himself claimed to have discovered an island of the Antilles which, in the words of Bartolomé de Las Casas, 'was inhabited solely by women, who are visited by the men at a certain time of the year; and if they bear a female child they keep it with them, if a male they send it away to the island of the men'. He believed that he had come across the source of the classical Greek myth of the Amazons. Before Orellana set out and during the early stages of his voyage he came across constant stories from the Indians of tribes whose women were trained to battle. Gaspar de Carbajal, who wrote a Diary of the voyage, reports an encounter they had with Indians on St John the Baptist's day, 1542.

'Here were seen Indian women with bows and arrows who fought as vigorously, or more so, than the men and goaded on the men to fight. They acted as leaders, took the foremost place in the battle, struck those who wished to flee and encouraged the others to do battle. What is certain is that these women, who fought like

Amazons, are the source of the stories widely disseminated among the Indians of a warlike race of women who have their kingdom somewhere in the district without commerce with men. . . They are tall and well built, go naked in war . . . but in peace they wear very comely mantles of thin cotton cloth.'

The myth had no firmer basis than the practice of certain tribes of the Amazon basin whose women took part in battle. Stories of these current among the Indians of Peru reached the Spaniards, who misunderstood their informants and too readily associated the rumours with the Greek myth. Carbajal himself says: 'We obtained many intimations about these women during all the voyage and even before we left the domains of Gonzalo Pizarro the existence of a kingdom of women was regarded as certain. But we improperly called them "Amazons" among ourselves.' In Chapter 86 of his *Historia General de las Indias* Gomara says:

'Among the nonsense he spoke he [Orellana] affirmed that there are Amazons on this river, with whom he and his comrades fought. That some of the women there carry arms and fight is a small matter, for this they

are accustomed to do in many parts of the Indies. But I don't believe that any woman cuts or burns off her right breast in order to be able to draw the bow, for they can do this quite well without. Nor do they kill or deport their male children or live without husbands. Others besides Orellana

Above right. A tiny but finely wrought gold figure of a man wearing a visored helmet and a semicircular headdress. It was possibly worn as a decoration (it is scarcely two and a half inches high), probably by a chieftain or a warrior. Tairona culture of the north-east coast of Colombia. Dumbarton Oaks, Washington D.C. Robert Woods Bliss Collection.

Right. A Quimbaya gold figure from Colombia, possibly an amulet. Little is known of this culture beyond its existence between the Cauca and Magdalena rivers at the time the Spaniards arrived in the New World. Gold work in this style has been discovered as far north as Panama. Cleveland Museum of Art, Ohio.

Opposite. A procession of small figures in silver found in a grave of the Inca period in the Chicama valley in Peru. It is believed to represent a funeral procession: the container preceding the litter (which probably carried the body) would have held the material belongings which were also interred. American Museum of Natural History, New York.

have bruited such stories of Amazons since the discovery of the Indies but no such has been seen or ever will be seen along this river. But it is these reports which cause many to speak of it as the "river of the Amazons".'

El Dorado

It was in the early stages of the conquest of the New World that Spanish explorers first heard from native tribes on the fringes of Central America whispered stories of a mysterious people in the south whose cities were paved and palaced in solid gold and of a kingdom ruled over by a mighty priest-king, called El Dorado – the Gilded Man – because his body was covered in powdered gold. There is no reasonable doubt that these stories were garbled and misunderstood accounts of the Inca, the fame of whose empire, percolating along the trade routes, had reverberated far beyond the ordered civilisation they had built up and was current among the more primitive peoples of the fringe in exaggerated

rumours of marvel and wonder. It was these stories which lured the Conquistadores to push south from Panama. Then having set themselves in the seat of the Inca and seized the Inca gold, they had achieved the goal they sought. But they did not recognise it for the goal and, with the reality already in their grasp, they still sought the illusion. For the legend of El Dorado persisted – and has persisted to this day – luring countless intrepid romantics to their death in the pathless jungles and fevered swamps of the Amazon valley, searching for the rumoured land of gold.

One of the most persistent rumours was centred about the mysterious Lake Guatavita, high in the mountains behind Santa Fé de Bogotá, into whose waters pieces of gold were cast as offerings to the god. From Gonzalo Ximenes de Quesada, who sought to recover the secret in 1569, roasting the local Chibcha chieftain over a slow fire, to the British company which in 1913 sank £15,000 in

a vain attempt to drain the lake, Guatavita has proved a will-o'-the-wisp to many sanguine hopes. There is a long list of those who perished in the forests beyond, seeking the country where the legendary gold of Guatavita had its origin.

No less tempting proved the fabulous country of Manoa or Omoa, located in the unexplored hinterland of the river Orinoco near the mythical Lake Parima, which was marked in maps of South America on the borders of Venezuela and Guiana until its existence was disproved by von Humboldt. Among the most famous expeditions in search of the El Dorado of the Omaguas, as it was called, was that of Diego de Ortaz in 1537. One of his men, a certain Juan Martínez, who became separated from his companions, reappeared many years later from the jungle, exhausted and emaciated, and swore on his deathbed that he had been entertained by El Dorado himself. In 1541-5 the expedition of Philip von Hutten followed the trail of the old

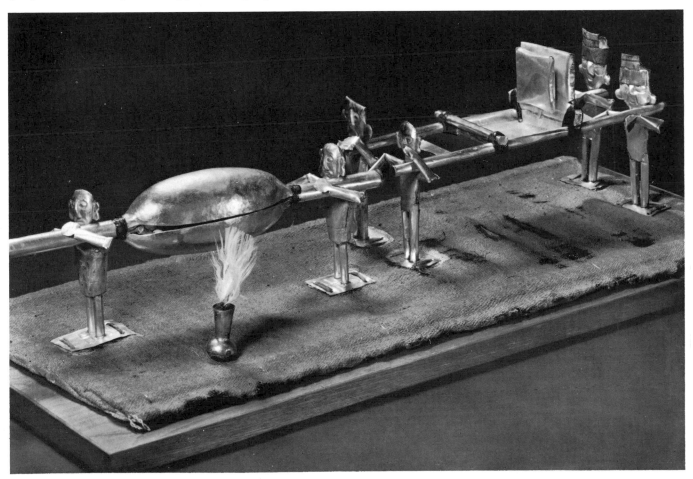

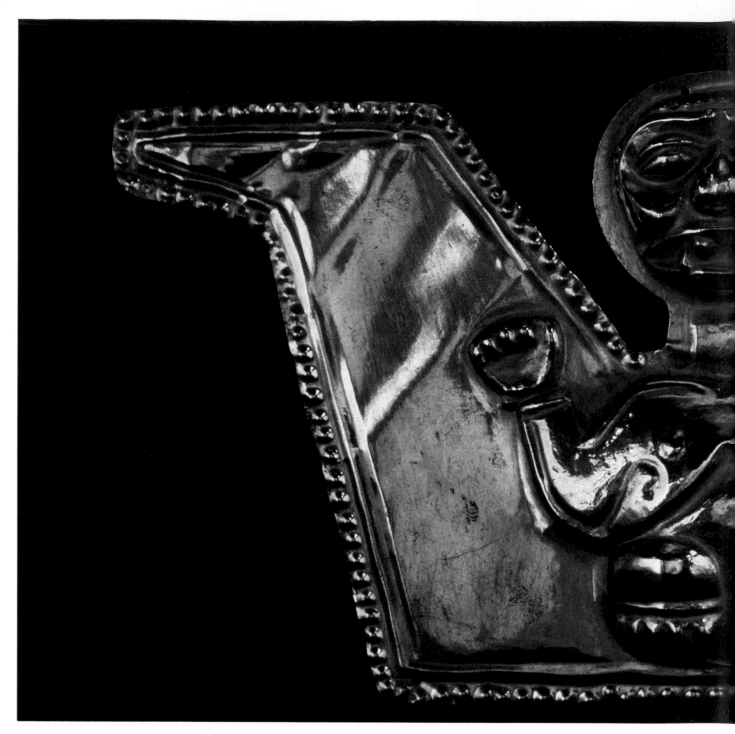

German knight Georg von Speier into the country beyond the Putumayo, a river later to become infamous as the scene of the worst atrocities of the rubber boom. In 1595 Sir Walter Raleigh declared his faith in the legend, hoping to renew the search.

All the expeditions into the Amazonian basin – and they were many – came upon rumours of El Dorado among the native tribes, rumours which directed them always a little further on. What they did not realise

was that these rumours were tribal lore handed down from generation to generation which had their origin in the fame of the great empire of the Inca at Cuzco – whence many of the expeditions of discovery had come. Though they did not know it, they were being directed back to the point of their departure.

The myth was also current among the Guaraní Indians of the Rio de la Plata basin. At the end of the fifteenth century bands of Guaraní raided ac-

ross the Chaco and brought back silver and gold looted from the peaceful tribes within the Inca empire. From this arose the rumour of a 'people of metal' far in the north, the Sierra de Plata. The myth of Paititi, the land of gold, ruled over by El Gran Moxo (the Musu of Quechua legend) became indigenous in Paraguay. It was supposed to be situated in a magic lake Cuni-Cuni at the sources of the river Paraguay and guarded by the jaguar-lizard, Teyú-Yaguá. When

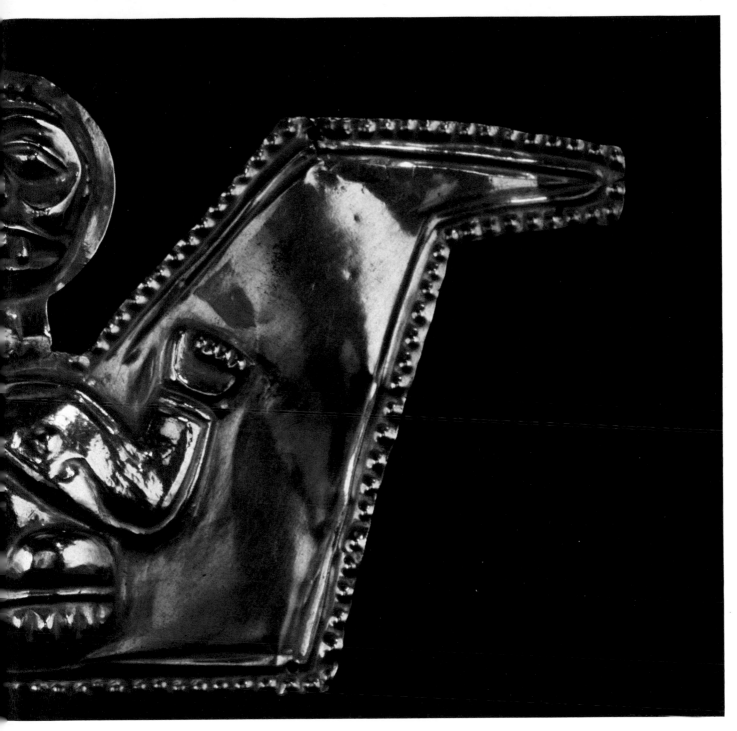

Gold plaque from Ecuador depicting a bat deity or personification. University Museum, Philadelphia, Pennsylvania.

Sebastian Cabot landed at Pernambuco in 1526 he heard these rumours from companions of an earlier adventurer Alejo García, stories of Indians who lived east of the Cordillera of Charcas and who 'wore silver crowns on their heads and gold plates hanging from their necks and ears and attached round their belts'. Convinced that this was El Dorado, Cabot sailed the Paraná and then the river Paraguay to its junction with the Pilcomayo.

Although his expedition was a failure, reports of the Quechua Indians of the Inca empire who traded gold and silver with the Guaraní continued to incite the covetousness of the Spaniards. In 1536 the Adelantado Pedro de Mendoza sent Juan de Ayloas with an expedition up the Paraguay and across the Chaco in search of the Caracaras (i.e. Quechuas of the Charcas). In 1553 Nuñez Cabeza de Vaca sent a certain Hernando de Ribera up the Paraguay and in the marshes of Xaragues at the entrance to Chiquitos the latter came across Inca trade goods and brought back the usual stories of a great and powerful people to the north-west, a land of gold and unlimited wealth, a country of Amazons, a race of white Indians and the land of El Dorado. Curiously enough the Spanish already established on the Altiplano got rumours of these stories and in turn believed that El Dorado lay to their east in the lowlands of Mojos. Expeditions from Sucre into Mojos were led by Lorenzo de Figueroa in 1580 and by Gonzalo de Solis de Holguín in 1617 and 1624.

The Chilean folklorist Julio Vicuña Cifuentes reports a legend of a magical city of gold, another version of the El Dorado myth, which he declares to be widespread in Chile. In the south of Chile on the borders of a mountain lake whose whereabouts no one knows there exists a magic city whose streets and palaces are of solid gold. The inhabitants are ideally happy, do not have to work to support themselves and live for ever. The city is invisible. Travellers who come upon it forget all about it after they leave and cannot remember the way back to it. Its church has a great bell so large that if it were to be rung it would be heard the whole world over. There is there an inexhaustible tobacco plantation. The people never travel from it. This golden city will become visible only at the end of the world. It is commonly known as the City of Caesars.

The name derives from Francisco César who, sponsored by Cabot, led an expedition of fourteen men to discover the land of gold in the interior. It is supposed that the Chilean myth combines memories of the fame of the Incas with features from the mythical abode of the dead and with memories of the expedition of César.

A gold plaque from Ecuador decorated with four feline figures. Musée de l'Homme.

A stirrup vase from the middle period of
the Mochica culture, apparently
expressing in a different vein the symbols
which recur again and again and which
suggest a priest and a feline cult. It is
quite possible that the creatures painted
on the ascending spiral are decoration
merely; but these together with the
elaborately dressed figure at the top
suggest something more.
Nathan Cummings, Chicago.

Further Reading List

Avila, Father Francisco de. *A Narrative of the Errors, False Gods, and other Superstitions and Diabolical Rites in which the Indians of Huarochiri lived in Ancient Times.* Translated and edited by Clements R. Markham in 'Rites and Laws of the Yncas'. Hakluyt Society, London, 1873.

Baudin, Louis. *A Socialist Empire: The Incas of Peru.* Princeton, New Jersey, 1961.

Baumann, Hans. *Gold and Gods of Peru.* Oxford University Press, London, 1963.

Bellamy, H. S. and Allen, Peter. *The Calendar of Tiahuanaco.* Faber and Faber, London, 1956.

Bushnell, G. H. S. *The Ancient People of the Andes.* Penguin Books, London and Harmondsworth, 1949.

Bushnell, G. H. S. *The Arts of the Ancient Americas.* Thames and Hudson, London, 1965.

Bushnell, G. H. S. *Peru.* Thames and Hudson. London. 1956.

Camara Cascudo, Luiz da. *Mitos Brasileiros.* Ed. Ministerio da Eduaçao e Cultura, Rio de Janeiro.

Cieza de León, Pedro de. *The Travels of Pedro de Cieza de León, Contained in the First Part of his Chronicle of Peru, AD 1532-1550.* No. 33, Hakluyt Society, London, 1864.

Cieza de León, Pedro de. *The Second Part of the Chronicle of Peru.* No. 68, Hakluyt Society, London, 1883.

Flornoy, Bertrand. *Inca Adventure.* Allen and Unwin, London, 1956.

Flornoy, Bertrand. *The World of the Inca.* Vanguard Press, New York, 1957.

Guppy, Nicholas. *Wai-Wai: Through the Forests North of the Amazon.* Dutton, Inc. New York, 1958.

Hagen, Victor W. von. *The Ancient Sun Kingdoms.* Thames and Hudson, London, 1962.

Hagen, Victor W. von. *The Desert Kingdoms of Peru.* Weidenfeld and Nicolson, London, 1965.

Kirkpatrick, A. *The Spanish Conquistadores.* A. & C. Black, London, 1946.

Lara, Jesus. *La Literatura de los Quechuas.* Editorial Canelas, Cochabamba, 1961.

Leicht, Hermann. *Pre-Inca Art and Culture.* MacGibbon and Kee, London, 1960.

MacCullough, John A. and Gray, Louis H. *The Mythology of All Races.* 13 vols, Cooper Square Pubs. Inc. New York, 1922.

Mason, John Alden. *The Ancient Civilisation of Peru.* Penguin Books, Harmondsworth, 1957.

Molina (of Cuzco), Cristóbal de. *The Fables and Rites of the Yncas* translated and edited by Clements R. Markham in 'Rites and Laws of the Yncas'. p. 1-64. Hakluyt Society, London, 1873.

Oblitas Poblete, Enrique. *Cultura Callawaya.* Ediciones Carmalinghi, La Paz, 1978.

Owens, R. J. *Peru.* Oxford University Press, London 1963.

Picon Salas, Mariano. *A Cultural History of South America.* University of California Press, Los Angeles, 1965.

Prescott, William Hickling. *History of the Conquest of Peru,* Everyman Library, London, 1963.

Rigoberto Parades, M. *Mitos, Supersticiones y supervivencias Populares de Bolivia.* Ediciones Isla, La Paz, 3rd ed, 1963.

Steward, Julian H. (editor). *Handbook of South American Indians.* Smithsonian Institution, Bureau of American Ethnology, Bulletin 143, vols, 2, 5, and 6, Washington, 1946-50.

Steward, Julian H. and Faron, Louis C. *Native Peoples of South America.* McGraw-Hill, New York, 1959.

Tchiffely, A. S. *Coricancha.* Hodder and Stoughton, London, 1949.

Varas Reyes, Vicot. *Huinaypacha.* Editorial America, Cochabamba, 1947.

Vicuña Cifuentes, Julio. *Mitos y supersticiones.* Editorial Nascimento, Santiago, 1947.

Acknowledgments

Photographs. American Museum of Natural History, New York half-title, 40, 42, 108 left, 133, 137; Mike Andrews, Bristol 16, 20 bottom, 41 top left; Ferdinand Anton, Munich 29, 73, 107; Art Institute of Chicago, Illinois 74 left, 104, 132 top; Bavaria Verlag, Gauting 89, 113; British Museum, London frontispiece 106; Camera Press, London 11, 41 bottom, 64 bottom right, 120; Cleveland Museum of Art, Ohio 55, 136 bottom; Deutsche Fotothek, Dresden 61; Dumbarton Oaks, Washington D.C. 26, 41 top right, 74 right, 96, 108 right, 129 right, 136 top; Arpad Elfer 46; Les Films du Château, Paris 72, 129 left; Giraudon 141; Hamlyn Group Picture Library 23, 24, 27, 31, 36 left, 36 centre, 37, 47, 49 top left, 49 top right, 49 bottom left, 49 bottom right, 53 top left, 53 top right, 53 bottom left, 53 bottom right, 54 left, 59, 60, 64 left, 69 bottom, 75, 78, 79, 81 left, 81 right, 85, 88, 91, 93, 94, 101, 103, 109, 116, 126, 132 bottom; Stephen Harrison, London 8 right; Hispanic & Luso Brazilian Council, London 65; Michael Holford, Loughton 18 top, 18 bottom, 19, 70, 86-87, 123; E. Kusch, Nuremberg 10-11, 17 left, 20 top right, 36 right, 48, 64 top right; Tony Morrison, Woodbridge 66, 77; Musée de l'Homme, Paris 22, 28, 43 left, 43 right, 80, 92 left, 111, 114-115, 121, 140; Museo Nacional de Antropologia y Arqueologia, Lima 128; Museum für Völkerunde, Berlin 52, 112; Museum of Archaeology and Ethnology, Cambridge 67, 102; Museum Rietberg, Zurich 105; Museum Rietberg, Zurich – Wettstein & Kauf 10 top, 71, 98, 99, 131 right, 134; H. Osborne 33, 100; Photoresources, Dover 35, 39, 54 right, 82, 83, 131 left; Paul Popper, London 44, 68; Réalités, Paris 7, 14, 15; Harald Schultz 12, 13 bottom, 122, 127, 130, 135; J.-C. Spahni, Geneva 8 left, 9, 13 top, 17 top right, 17 bottom right, 20 top left, 32, 43, 56, 57, 69 top, 92 right, 97, 125; Staatliche Museum für Völkerkunde, Munich 118 top left, 118 top right, 118 bottom, 119; University Museum, Philadelphia, Pennsylvania 50-51, 62-63, 138-139; Roger-Viollet, paris 24-25.

Index